DK EYEWITNESS TRAVEL

15-MINUTE
SPANISH

DK EYEWITNESS TRAVEL

15-MINUTE
SPANISH

LEARN SPANISH IN JUST 15 MINUTES A DAY

ANA BREMÓN

London, New York, Munich, Melbourne,
and Delhi

Dorling Kindersley Limited
Senior Editor Angeles Gavira
Project Art Editor Vanessa Marr
DTP Designer John Goldsmid
Production Controller Luca Frassinetti
Publishing Manager Liz Wheeler
Managing Art Editor Philip Ormerod
Publishing Director Jonathan Metcalf
Art Director Bryn Walls

Language content for Dorling Kindersley by
g-and-w publishing

Produced for Dorling Kindersley by
Schermuly Design Co.
Art Editor Hugh Schermuly
Project Editor Cathy Meeus
Special photography Mike Good

First American Edition, 2005
Published in the United States by
DK Publishing, Inc., 375 Hudson Street,
New York, New York 10014

05 06 07 08 09   10 9 8 7 6 5 4 3 2

A Cataloging-in-Publication record for this book
is available from the Library of Congress.

ISBN 0-7566-0920-8

15-Minute Spanish is also available in a pack
with two CDs
ISBN 0-7566-0927-5

Color reproduction by Colourscan, Singapore
Printed and bound in China by Leo Paper
Products Limited

Discover more at
www.dk.com

Contents

How to use this book 6

Week 1
Introductions

Week 2
Eating and drinking

Week 3
Making arrangements

Week 4
Travel

How to use this book

This main part of the book is devoted to 12 themed chapters, broken down into five 15-minute daily lessons, the last of which is a revision lesson. So, in just 12 weeks you will have completed the course. A concluding reference section contains a menu guide and English-to-Spanish and Spanish-to-English dictionaries.

Warm up and clock
Each day starts with a one-minute warm-up that encourages you to recall vocabulary or phrases you have learned previously. A clock to the right of the heading bar indicates the amount of time you are expected to spend on each exercise.

Instructions
Each exercise is numbered and introduced by instructions that explain what to do. In some cases additional information is given about the language point being covered.

Cultural/Conversational tip
These panels provide additional insights into life in Spain and language usage.

Text styles
Distinctive text styles differentiate Spanish and English, and the pronunciation guide (see right).

How to use the flap
The book's cover flaps allow you to conceal the Spanish so that you can test whether you have remembered correctly.

Revision pages
A recap of selected elements of previous lessons helps to reinforce your knowledge.

In conversation
Illustrated dialogues reflecting how vocabulary and phrases are used in everyday situations appear throughout the book.

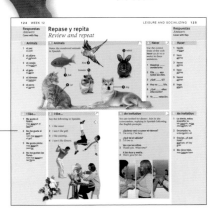

Useful phrases
Selected phrases relevant to the topic help you speak and understand.

EATING AND DRINKING 19

Useful phrases

Learn these phrases. Read the English under the picture and say the phrase in Spanish as shown on the right. Then cover the Spanish with the flap and test yourself.

los churros
los choorros
churros

el azúcar
el athookar
sugar

el café con leche
el kafeh kon lecheh
coffee with milk

Me pone un café.
meh poneh oon kafeh
I'll have a black coffee.

¿Eso es todo?
esoh es todoh
Is that all?

Yo voy a tomar churros.
yoh boy a tomar choorros
I'm going to have some churros.

¿Cuánto es?
kwantoh es
How much is that?

l, señor.
n, senyor
..., sir

Gracias. ¿Cuánto es?
grathyas. kwantoh es
Thank you. How much is that?

Cuatro euros, por favor.
kwatroh ewros, por fabor
Four euros, please.

Pronunciation guide

This book teaches European Spanish, which differs in pronunciation from the various dialects spoken in Latin America. A few Spanish sounds require special explanation:

c a Spanish **c** is pronounced *th* before **i** or **e** but **k** before other vowels: **cinco** <u>theen</u>koh (*five*)

h **h** is always silent: **hola** o-lah (*hello*)

j (g) a Spanish **j** (and **g** before **i** or **e**) is pronounced as a strong *h*, as if saying <u>hat</u> emphazing the first letter

ll pronounced *y* as in *yes*

ñ pronounced *ny* like the sound in the middle of *canyon*

r a Spanish **r** is trilled like a Scottish **r**, especially at the beginning of a word and when doubled

v a Spanish **v** is halfway between an English *b* and *v*

z a Spanish **z** is pronounced *th*

Spanish vowels tend to be pronounced shorter than their English equivalents:

a as the English *father*
e as the English *wet*
i as the English *keep*
o as the English *boat*
u as the English *boot*

After each word or phrase you will find a pronunciation transcription, with underlining showing the stress. Remember that this can only be an approximation; there is no substitute for listening to and mimicking native speakers.

Say it
In these exercises you are asked to apply what you have learned using different vocabulary.

5 Say it

Do you have a single room, please?

For six nights.

Is breakfast included?

Dictionary
A mini-dictionary provides ready reference from English to Spanish and Spanish to English for 2,500 words.

132 DICTIONARY

Dictionary
English to Spanish

The gender of a Spanish noun is indicated by the word for the **el** and **la** (masculine and feminine singular) or their plural form **los** (masculine) and **las** (feminine). Spanish adjectives (adj) vary according to the gender and number of the word they describe, and the masculine form is shown here. In general, adjectives that end in **-o** adopt an **-a** ending in the feminine form, and those that end in **-e** usually stay the same. For the plural form, an **-s** is added.

128 MENU GUIDE

Menu guide
This guide lists the most common terms you may encounter on Spanish menus or when shopping for food. If you can't find an exact phrase, try looking up its component parts.

Menu guide
Use this guide as a reference for food terminology and popular Spanish dishes.

1 Warm up

The Warm Up appears at the beginning of each lesson. It will remind you of what you have already learned and prepare you for moving ahead with the new subject.

Hola
Hello

In Spain, women often greet each other with one or two kisses on the cheek, and men shake other men's hands, although men may kiss or embrace younger male relatives or close friends. In formal situations— among strangers or in a business context—a handshake is the norm.

2 Words to remember

Look at these greetings and say them aloud. Conceal the text on the left with the cover flap and try to remember the Spanish for each item. Check your answers.

¡Hola!
o-lah
Hello!

Buenos días. bwenos deeyas	*Good morning/day.*
Me llamo Ana. may yamoh anna	*My name is Ana.*
Encantado/-a. enkan-tadoh/-ah	*Pleased to meet you (man/woman speaking).*
Buenas tardes (noches). bwenas tardes (noches)	*Good afternoon/ evening (night).*

Cultural tip The Spanish frequently address people as "señor" (sir), "señora" (madam, for older women), and "señorita" (miss, for young women). With first names use "Don" for men or "Doña" for women: Don Juan, Doña Ana.

3 In conversation: formal

Buenos días. Me llamo Concha García.
bwenos deeyas. may yamoh konchah garthee-ah

Good day. My name is Concha García.

Señor López, encantado.
senyor lopeth, enkan-tadoh

Mr. López, pleased to meet you.

Encantada.
enkan-tadah

Pleased to meet you.

4 Put into practice

Join in this conversation. Read the Spanish beside the pictures on the left and then follow the instructions to make your reply. Then test yourself by concealing the answers on the right with the cover flap.

Buenas tardes señor.
<u>bwe</u>nas <u>tar</u>des sen<u>yor</u>
Good evening, sir.

Say: Good evening, madam.

Buenas tardes señora.
<u>bwe</u>nas <u>tar</u>des sen<u>yo</u>rah

Me llamo Julia.
may <u>ya</u>moh <u>hoo</u>lya
My name is Julia.

Say: Pleased to meet you.

Encantado.
enkan-<u>ta</u>doh

5 Useful phrases

Read these phrases aloud several times and try to memorize them. Conceal the Spanish with the cover flap and test yourself.

What's your name?	**¿Cómo se llama?** <u>ko</u>mo seh <u>ya</u>mah
Goodbye.	**Adiós.** addy-<u>os</u>
Thank you.	**Gracias.** <u>grath</u>yas
See you soon/ tomorrow.	**Hasta pronto/mañana.** <u>as</u>tah <u>pron</u>toh/ man<u>ya</u>nah

6 In conversation: informal

Entonces, ¿hasta mañana?
en<u>ton</u>thes, <u>as</u>tah man<u>ya</u>nah

So, see you tomorrow?

Sí, adiós.
see, addy-<u>os</u>

Yes, goodbye.

Adiós. Hasta pronto.
addy-<u>os</u>. <u>as</u>tah <u>pron</u>toh

Goodbye. See you soon.

1 Warm up

Say "hello" and "goodbye" in Spanish. (pp.8–9)

Now say "My name is...". (pp.8–9)

Say "sir" and "madam." (pp.8–9)

Las relaciones
Relatives

The Spanish equivalents of *mom* and *dad* are **mamá** and **papá**. The male plural can refer to both sexes—for example, **niños** (*boys* and *children*), **padres** (*fathers* and *parents*), **abuelos** (*grandfathers* and *grandparents*), **tíos** (*uncles* and *aunt and uncle*), **hermanos** (*brothers* and *siblings*), and so on.

2 Match and repeat

Look at the people in this scene and match their numbers with the list at the side. Read the Spanish words aloud. Then conceal the list with the cover flap and test yourself.

1 **la hermana**
lah air<u>ma</u>nah

2 **el abuelo**
el a<u>bwe</u>loh

3 **el padre**
el <u>pah</u>dray

4 **el hermano**
el air<u>ma</u>noh

5 **la abuela**
lah a<u>bwe</u>lah

6 **la hija**
lah <u>ee</u>-hah

7 **la madre**
lah <u>mah</u>dray

8 **el hijo**
el <u>ee</u>-hoh

❶ *sister*

❷ *grandfather*

❸ *father*

❹ *brother*

❺ *grandmother*

❻ *daughter*

❼ *mother*

❽ *son*

Conversational tip In Spanish, things as well as people are masculine or feminine—for example, "wine" is masculine ("el vino") but "milk" is feminine ("la leche"). Use "los" and "las" for masculine and feminine plurals, respectively. For "a/an," use "un" for masculine and "una" for feminine items.

3 Words to remember: relatives

Familiarize yourself with these words. Read them aloud several times and try to memorize them. Conceal the Spanish with the cover flap and test yourself.

el marido
el ma<u>ree</u>doh
husband

la mujer
lah moo-<u>hair</u>
wife

Estoy casado/-a.
es<u>toy</u> ka<u>sa</u>doh/-ah
I'm married (m/f).

father/mother-in-law	**el suegro/la suegra** el <u>swe</u>groh/lah <u>swe</u>grah
stepfather	**el padrastro** el pa<u>dras</u>-troh
stepmother	**la madrastra** lah ma<u>dras</u>-trah
children (male/female)	**los niños/las niñas** los <u>nee</u>nyos/las <u>nee</u>nyas
uncle/aunt	**el tío/la tía** lah <u>tee</u>-ah/el <u>tee</u>-oh
cousin	**el primo/la prima** el <u>pree</u>moh/lah <u>pree</u>mah
I have four children.	**Tengo cuatro niños.** <u>ten</u>goh <u>kwa</u>troh <u>nee</u>nyos
I have two stepdaughters and a stepson.	**Tengo dos hijastras y un hijastro.** <u>ten</u>goh dos ee-<u>has</u>tras ee oon ee-<u>has</u>troh

4 Words to remember: numbers

Memorize these words and then test yourself using the cover flap.

Be careful when you use the number one. When you use **uno** in front of a word, it changes to **un** or **una**, depending on whether that word is masculine or feminine. For example: **Tengo un hijo** (*I have one son*), **Tengo una hija** (*I have one daughter*).

one	**uno/-a** <u>oo</u>noh/-ah
two	**dos** dos
three	**tres** tres
four	**cuatro** <u>kwa</u>troh
five	**cinco** <u>theen</u>koh
six	**seis** seys
seven	**siete** <u>sye</u>tay
eight	**ocho** <u>o</u>choh
nine	**nueve** <u>nwe</u>bay
ten	**diez** d<u>yeth</u>

5 Say it

I have five sons.

I have three sisters and a brother.

I have two children.

1 Warm up

Say the Spanish for as many members of the family as you can. (pp.10–11)

Say "I have two sons." (pp.10–11)

Mi familia
My family

There are two ways of saying *you* in Spanish, **usted** for formal situations and **tú** in informal ones. There is also a formal way of saying *your*—**su** (singular) and **sus** (plural): **usted y su mujer** (*you and your wife*), **¿Son ésos sus hijos?** (*Are those your sons?*). **Su** and **sus** also mean *his* and *her*.

2 Words to remember

Say these words aloud a few times. Conceal the Spanish with the cover flap and try to remember the Spanish word for each item.

mi mee	*my (with singular)*
mis mees	*my (with plural)*
tu too	*your (informal with singular)*
tus toos	*your (informal with plural)*
su soo	*your (formal with singular)*
sus soos	*your (formal with plural)*
su soo	*his/her (with singular) their (with singular)*
sus soos	*his/her (with plural) their (with plural)*

Éstos son mis padres.
<u>es</u>tos son mees <u>pah</u>dres
These are my parents.

3 In conversation

¿Tiene usted niños?
<u>tye</u>nay oos<u>ted</u> <u>neen</u>yos

Do you have any children?

Sí, tengo dos hijas.
see, <u>ten</u>goh dos <u>ee</u>-has

Yes, I have two daughters.

Éstas son mis hijas. ¿Y usted?
<u>es</u>tas son mees <u>ee</u>-has. ee oos<u>ted</u>

These are my daughters. And you?

Conversational tip The Spanish ask a question by simply raising the pitch of the voice at the end of a statement: "¿Quieres un poco de vino?" ("Do you want a little wine?"). Notice the upside-down question mark (¿) written at the beginning of the question. You will also see an upside-down exclamation mark, as in "¡Hola!" ("Hello!").

4 Useful phrases

Read these phrases aloud several times and try to memorize them. Conceal the Spanish with the cover flap and test yourself.

	Do you have any brothers? (formal)	**¿Tiene usted hermanos?** tyenay oosted airmanos
	Do you have any brothers? (informal)	**¿Tienes hermanos?** tyenes airmanos
	This is my husband.	**Éste es mi marido.** estay es mee mareedoh
	That's my wife.	**Ésa es mi mujer.** esah es mee moo-hair
	Is that your sister? (formal)	**¿Es ésa su hermana?** es esah soo airmanah
	Is that your sister? (informal)	**¿Es ésa tu hermana?** es esah too airmanah

No, pero tengo un hijastro.
noh, peroh tengoh oon ee-hastroh

No, but I have a stepson.

5 Say it

Do you have any brothers and sisters? (formal)

Do you have any children? (informal)

I have two sisters.

This is my wife, María.

1 Warm up

Say "See you soon."
(pp.8–9)

Say "I am married"
(pp.10–11) and
"I have a wife."
(pp.12–13)

Ser y tener
To be and to have

Two of the most important verbs are
ser (*to be*) and **tener** (*to have*). Note that
there are different ways of saying *you*,
we, and *they*, with formal and
informal, singular and plural, and
masculine and feminine forms.
Pronouns (*I, you*, etc.) are omitted
where the sense is clear.

2 Ser: to be

Familiarize yourself with **ser** (*to be*). When you are confident, practice
the sample sentences below. Note: there is another verb meaning "to
be"—**estar**, which is discussed on page 49.

yo soy yoh soy	*I am*
tú eres too <u>eh</u>-res	*you are (informal singular)*
usted es oosted es	*you are (formal singular)*
él/ella es el/<u>eh</u>-yah es	*he/she is*
nosotros/-as somos no<u>so</u>tros/-as <u>so</u>mos	*we are (masculine/feminine)*
vosotros/-as sois bo<u>so</u>tros/-as soys	*you are (informal plural, m/f)*
ustedes son oos<u>te</u>des son	*you are (formal plural)*
ellos/-as son eh-yos/-yas son	*they are (masculine/feminine)*

Yo soy inglesa.
yoh soy eengl<u>e</u>sah
I'm English.

¿De dónde es usted? day <u>don</u>day es oos<u>ted</u>	*Where are you from?*
Es mi hermana. es mee air<u>ma</u>nah	*She is my sister.*
Somos españoles. <u>so</u>mos espany<u>o</u>les	*We're Spanish.*

3 Tener: to have

Practice **tener** (*to have*) and the sample sentences, then test yourself.

I have	**yo tengo**	yoh <u>ten</u>goh
you have (*informal singular*)	**tú tienes**	too <u>tye</u>nes
you have (*formal singular*)	**usted tiene**	oosted <u>tye</u>nay
he/she has	**él/ella tiene**	el/<u>eh</u>-yah <u>tye</u>nay
we have (*masculine/feminine*)	**nosotros/-as tenemos**	no<u>so</u>tros/-as te<u>nay</u>mos
you have (*informal plural, m/f*)	**vosotros/-as teneis**	bo<u>so</u>tros/-as te<u>nay</u>s
you have (*formal plural*)	**ustedes tienen**	oos<u>te</u>des <u>tye</u>nen
they have (*masculine/feminine*)	**ellos/-as tienen**	<u>eh</u>-yos/-yas <u>tye</u>nen

¿Tiene rosas rojas?
<u>tye</u>nay <u>ro</u>sas <u>ro</u>has
Do you have red roses?

He has a meeting.	**Tiene una reunión.**	<u>tye</u>nay <u>oo</u>nah re-oony<u>on</u>
Do you have a cell phone?	**¿Tiene usted móvil?**	<u>tye</u>nay oosted <u>mo</u>beel?
How many brothers and sisters do you have?	**¿Cuántos hermanos tiene usted?**	k<u>wan</u>tos air<u>ma</u>nos <u>tye</u>nay oos<u>ted</u>

4 Negatives

It is easy to make sentences negative in Spanish; just put **no** in front of the verb: **No somos americanos** (*We're not American*).

la bicicleta
lah beethee<u>kle</u>tah
bicycle

I'm not Spanish.	**No soy español.**	noh soy espany<u>ol</u>
He's not a vegetarian.	**No es vegetariano.**	noh es be-hetary<u>a</u>noh
We don't have any children.	**No tenemos niños.**	noh te<u>nay</u>mos <u>nee</u>nyos

No tengo coche.
noh <u>ten</u>goh <u>ko</u>chay
I don't have a car.

Repase y repita
Review and repeat

Respuestas
Answers
Cover with flap

1 How many?

1 **tres**
tres

2 **nueve**
<u>nwe</u>bay

3 **cuatro**
<u>kwa</u>troh

4 **dos**
dos

5 **ocho**
<u>o</u>choh

6 **diez**
<u>dye</u>th

7 **cinco**
<u>theen</u>koh

8 **siete**
<u>sye</u>tay

9 **six**
seys

1 How many?

Cover the answers with the flap. Then say these Spanish numbers out loud. Check to see if you remembered the Spanish correctly.

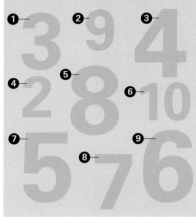

2 Hello

1 **Buenos días. Me llamo... [your name].**
<u>bwe</u>nos <u>dee</u>yas.
may <u>ya</u>moh...

2 **Encantado/-a.**
enkan-<u>ta</u>doh/-ah

3 **Sí, y tengo dos hijos. ¿Y usted?**
see, ee <u>ten</u>goh dos <u>ee</u>-hos. ee oos<u>ted</u>

4 **Adiós. Hasta mañana.**
addy-<u>os</u>. <u>as</u>tah man<u>ya</u>nah

2 Hello

You are talking to someone you have just met. Join in the conversation, replying in Spanish following the English prompts.

Buenos días. Me llamo María.
1 *Answer the greeting and give your name.*

Éste es mi marido, Juan.
2 *Say "Pleased to meet you."*

¿Está usted casado/-a?
3 *Say "Yes, and I have two sons. And you?"*

Nosotros tenemos tres hijos.
4 *Say "Goodbye. See you tomorrow."*

3 To have or be

Fill in the blanks with the correct form of **tener** (*to have*) or **ser** (*to be*). Check to see if you have remembered the Spanish correctly.

1 Yo _____ americana.

2 Nosotros _____ cuatro niños.

3 Yo no _____ feliz.

4 ¿ _____ tú coche?

5 Él _____ mi marido.

6 Yo no _____ teléfono móvil.

7 Tú no _____ español.

8 ¿ _____ usted hijos?

3 To have or be

1 **soy**
soy

2 **tenemos**
te<u>nay</u>mos

3 **soy**
soy

4 **tienes**
<u>tye</u>nes

5 **es**
es

6 **tengo**
<u>tengoh</u>

7 **eres**
<u>eh</u>-res

8 **tiene**
<u>tye</u>nay

4 Family

Say the Spanish for each of the numbered family members. Check to see if you have remembered the Spanish correctly.

② *grandfather*

sister ①   ③ *father*

④ *brother*

⑥ *daughter*   ⑧ *son*

⑤ *grandmother*   ⑦ *mother*

4 Family

1 **la hermana**
lah air<u>ma</u>nah

2 **el abuelo**
el a<u>bwe</u>loh

3 **el padre**
el <u>pah</u>dray

4 **el hermano**
el air<u>ma</u>noh

5 **la abuela**
lah a<u>bwe</u>lah

6 **la hija**
lah <u>ee</u>-hah

7 **la madre**
lah <u>mah</u>dray

8 **el hijo**
el <u>ee</u>-hoh

1 Warm up

Count to ten.
(pp.10–11)

Remind yourself how to say "hello" and "goodbye." (pp.8–9)

Ask "Do you have a son?" (pp.14–15)

En la cafetería
In the café

In a Spanish café you can get bread and pastries with your coffee in the mornings. **Churros** (fried dough sticks) are a typical Spanish snack. You can either sit at the counter or have waiter service at a table. It is normal to tip the waiter, but a few coins is usually enough.

2 Words to remember

Familiarize yourself with these words.

el té con limón el tay kon lee<u>mon</u>	*tea with lemon*
el café descafeinado el ka<u>fay</u> deskafey<u>nadoh</u>	*decaffeinated coffee*
el cortado el kor<u>tadoh</u>	*espresso with a bit of milk*
la mermelada lah merme<u>ladah</u>	*jam*
la tostada con mantequilla lah tos<u>tadah</u> kon mante<u>kee</u>-yah	*toast with butter*

el chocolate
el choko<u>latay</u>
hot chocolate

el café solo
el ka<u>fay</u> <u>soloh</u>
espresso

Cultural tip A standard coffee is small and black; if you want it any other way, you'll need to specify. If you want tea with milk, ask for "té con leche." If you just ask for "té," you are likely to get tea with lemon.

3 In conversation

Buenos días. Me pone un café con leche.
<u>bwenos</u> <u>deey</u>as. may <u>ponay</u> oon ka<u>fay</u> kon <u>lechay</u>

Hello. I'll have coffee with milk, please.

¿Eso es todo?
<u>esoh</u> es <u>todoh</u>

Is that all?

¿Tiene churros?
<u>tyenay</u> <u>choor</u>ros

Do you have any churros?

4 Useful phrases

Learn these phrases. Read the English under the pictures and say the phrase in Spanish as shown on the right. Then cover the Spanish with the flap and test yourself.

los churros
los <u>choo</u>rros
churros

el azúcar
el ah-<u>thoo</u>kar
sugar

el café con leche
el <u>kafay</u> kon <u>lechay</u>
coffee with milk

Me pone un café.
may <u>po</u>nay oon ka<u>fay</u>

I'll have a black coffee.

¿Eso es todo?
<u>e</u>soh es <u>to</u>doh

Is that all?

Yo voy a tomar churros.
yoh boy ah to<u>mar</u> <u>choo</u>rros

I'm going to have some churros.

¿Cuánto es?
<u>kwan</u>toh es

How much is that?

Sí, señor.
see, sen<u>yor</u>

Yes, sir.

Gracias. ¿Cuánto es?
<u>grath</u>yas. <u>kwan</u>toh es

Thank you. How much is that?

Cuatro euros, por favor.
<u>kwa</u>troh eh-<u>oo</u>ros, por fa<u>bor</u>

Four euros, please.

1 Warm up

Ask "How much is that?" (pp.18–19)

Say "I don't have a brother." (pp.14–15)

Ask "Do you have any churros?" (pp.18–19)

En el restaurante
In the restaurant

There are a variety of different types of eating places in Spain. In a **bar** or **tasca** you can find a few **tapas** or snacks. Lunch is the main meal of the day, but if you are not very hungry, many restaurants offer tapas at the bar, which is usually very economical for a light meal.

2 Words to remember

Memorize these words. Conceal the Spanish with the cover flap and test yourself.

cup **7**

la carta lah <u>kar</u>tah	*menu*
la carta de vinos lah <u>kar</u>tah day <u>bee</u>nos	*wine list*
los entrantes los en<u>tran</u>tes	*appetizers*
el plato principal el <u>pla</u>toh preen<u>thee</u>pal	*main course*
los postres los <u>pos</u>tres	*desserts*
el desayuno el desah-<u>yoo</u>noh	*breakfast*
el almuerzo el almoo<u>air</u>thoh	*lunch*
la cena lah <u>the</u>nah	*dinner*

knife **6**

5 *spoon* **4** *fork*

3 In conversation

Hola. Una mesa para cuatro, por favor.
<u>o</u>-lah. <u>oo</u>nah <u>me</u>sah <u>pa</u>rah <u>kwa</u>troh, por fa<u>bor</u>

Hello. A table for four, please.

¿Tiene una reserva?
<u>tye</u>nay <u>oo</u>nah re<u>ser</u>bah

Do you have a reservation?

Sí, a nombre de Cortés.
see, ah <u>nom</u>bray day kor<u>tes</u>

Yes, in the name of Cortés.

4 Match and repeat

Look at the numbered objects on this table and match them with
the items in the vocabulary list at the side. Read the Spanish words
aloud. Now, conceal the list with the cover flap and test yourself.

glass ❶

❽ *saucer*

napkin ❷

plate ❸

1 **la copa**
   lah <u>ko</u>pah

2 **la servilleta**
   lah serbee-<u>ye</u>tah

3 **el plato**
   el <u>pla</u>toh

4 **el tenedor**
   el tene<u>dor</u>

5 **la cuchara**
   lah koo<u>cha</u>rah

6 **el cuchillo**
   el koo<u>chee</u>-yoh

7 **la taza**
   lah <u>ta</u>thah

8 **el platillo**
   el pla<u>tee</u>yoh

5 Useful phrases

Learn these phrases and then test yourself
using the cover flap to conceal the Spanish.

What do you have for dessert?	**¿Qué tiene de postre?** kay <u>tye</u>nay day <u>pos</u>tray
The check, please.	**La cuenta, por favor.** lah <u>kwen</u>tah, por fa<u>bor</u>

¿Fumadores o no fumadores?
fooma<u>do</u>res oh noh
fooma<u>do</u>res

Smoking or nonsmoking?

No fumadores, por favor.
noh fooma<u>do</u>res, por
fa<u>bor</u>

Nonsmoking, please.

Síganme, por favor.
<u>see</u>gan-may, por fa<u>bor</u>.

Follow me, please.

Querer
To want

Querer (*to want*) is a verb that is essential to everyday conversation. There is also a polite form, **quisiera** (*I'd like*). Use this when requesting something because **quiero** (*I want*) may sound too strong: **¿Qué quiere beber?** (*What do you want to drink?*); **Quisiera una cerveza** (*I'd like a beer*).

2 Querer: to want

Say the different forms of **querer** (*to want*) aloud. Use the cover flap to test yourself and, when you are confident, practice the sample sentences below.

yo quiero yoh <u>kya</u>iroh	*I want*
tú quieres/usted quiere too <u>kya</u>ires/oosted <u>kya</u>iray	*you want (singular, informal/ formal)*
él/ella quiere el/<u>eh</u>-yah <u>kya</u>iray	*he/she wants*
nosotros/-as queremos no<u>so</u>tros/-as ke<u>ra</u>ymos	*we want (masculine/ feminine)*
vosotros/-as queréis/ ustedes quieren bo<u>so</u>tros/-as ke<u>ra</u>ys/ oos<u>te</u>des <u>kya</u>iren	*you want (plural, informal/ formal)*
ellos/-as quieren <u>eh</u>-yos/-as-yas <u>kya</u>iren	*they want (masculine/ feminine)*
¿Quieres vino? <u>kya</u>ires <u>bee</u>noh?	*Do you want some wine?*
Quiere un coche nuevo. <u>kya</u>iray oon <u>ko</u>chay <u>nwe</u>boh	*She wants a new car.*

Quiero caramelos.
<u>kya</u>iroh kara<u>me</u>los
I want some candy.

Conversational tip Although it may sound rude to you, Spaniards don't say "please" (por favor) or "thank you" (gracias) very often, and they hardly ever say "excuse me" (perdón) or "I'm sorry" (lo siento), but they use the tone of their voices and choice of words to imply politeness, such as "quisiera" (I'd like) instead of "quiero" (I want).

3 Polite requests

Practice the following sample phrases that use **quisiera** (*I'd like*), the form of **quiero** (*I want*) that is used for polite requests.

I'd like a beer.

Quisiera un cerveza.
kee<u>sy</u>airah oon
therbaythah

I'd like a table for tonight.

Quisiera una mesa para esta noche.
kee<u>sy</u>airah <u>oo</u>nah <u>me</u>sah <u>pa</u>rah <u>es</u>tah <u>no</u>cheh

I'd like to see the menu, please.

Quisiera ver la carta, por favor.
kee<u>sy</u>airah <u>ber</u> lah <u>kar</u>tah, por fa<u>bor</u>

4 Put into practice

Join in this conversation. Read the Spanish beside the pictures on the left and follow the instructions to make your reply. Then test yourself by concealing the answers using the cover flap.

Buenas tardes señor. ¿Tiene una reserva?
<u>bwe</u>nas <u>tar</u>des sen<u>yor</u>. <u>ty</u>eneh <u>oo</u>nah re<u>ser</u>bah
Good evening, sir. Do you have a reservation?

Say: No, but I would like a table for three.

No, pero quisiera una mesa para tres.
noh, <u>pe</u>roh kee<u>sy</u>airah <u>oo</u>nah <u>me</u>sah <u>pa</u>rah tres

Muy bien. ¿Qué mesa le gustaría?
mwee byen. kay <u>me</u>sah le goos<u>ta</u>reeyah
Fine. Which table would you like?

Say: Near the window, please.

Cerca de la ventana, por favor.
<u>ther</u>kah day lah ben<u>ta</u>nah, por fa<u>bor</u>

1 Warm up

Say "She's happy"
and "I'm not sure."
(pp.14–15)

Ask "Do you have
churros?" (pp.18–19)

Say "I'd like coffee
with milk." (pp.18–19)

Los platos
Dishes

Spain offers a large variety of regional
dishes. Plenty of garlic and olive oil
are a feature of many typical recipes.
Restaurants do not normally offer a
vegetarian menu; there are, however,
many traditional Spanish dishes that
do not contain any meat. Ask your
waiter for advice.

Cultural tip At lunch time, you will find many
restaurants offer "el menú del día" (the day's set
menu). This is usually a three-course meal with bread
and a drink included in the price.

2 Match and repeat

Match the numbered items to the Spanish words in the panel.

1 **las verduras**
las ber<u>doo</u>ras

2 **la fruta**
lah <u>froo</u>tah

3 **el queso**
el <u>kes</u>oh

4 **los frutos secos**
los <u>froo</u>tos <u>se</u>kos

5 **la sopa**
lah <u>so</u>pah

6 **las aves**
las <u>ah</u>bes

7 **el pescado**
el pes<u>ka</u>doh

8 **la pasta**
lah <u>pas</u>tah

9 **el marisco**
el ma<u>rees</u>koh

10 **la carne**
lah <u>kar</u>nay

1 vegetables

2 fruit

3 cheese

5 soup

6 poultry

8 pasta

9 seafood

3 Words to remember: cooking methods

The ending often varies depending on the gender of item described.

fried (m/f)	**frito/-a** <u>free</u>toh/-ah
grilled	**a la plancha** ah lah <u>plan</u>chah
roasted (m/f)	**asado/-a** ah<u>sa</u>doh/-ah
boiled (m/f)	**hervido/-a** er<u>bee</u>doh/-ah
steamed	**al vapor** al ba<u>por</u>
rare (m/f)	**poco hecho/-a** pokoh <u>eh</u>-choh/-ah

Quisiera mi filete bien hecho.
kee<u>sya</u>irah mee fee<u>le</u>tay byen <u>eh</u>-choh
I'd like my steak well done.

6 Say it

What is "tortilla"?

I'm allergic to seafood.

I'd like a beer.

4 Words to remember: drinks

Familiarize yourself with these words.

water	**el agua** el <u>ah</u>gwah
sparkling water	**el agua con gas** el <u>ah</u>gwah kon gas
still water	**el agua sin gas** el <u>ah</u>gwah seen gas
wine	**el vino** el <u>bee</u>noh
beer	**la cerveza** lah thair<u>bay</u>thah
fruit juice	**el zumo** el <u>thoo</u>moh

4 nuts

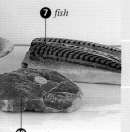

7 fish

5 Useful phrases

Learn these phrases and then test yourself.

I am a vegetarian (m/f).	**Soy vegetariano/-a.** soy be-hetar<u>eea</u>noh/-ah
I am allergic to nuts. (m/f)	**Soy alérgico/-a a los frutos secos.** soy ah<u>ler</u>-heekoh/-ah ah los <u>froo</u>tos <u>se</u>kos
What is "conejo"?	**¿Qué es "conejo"?** kay es ko<u>ne</u>-hoh

10 meat

Repase y repita
Review and repeat

1 What food?

1 **los frutos secos**
   los <u>froo</u>tos <u>se</u>kos

2 **el marisco**
   el mar<u>ee</u>skoh

3 **la carne**
   lah <u>kar</u>nay

4 **el azúcar**
   el ah-<u>thoo</u>kar

5 **la copa**
   lah <u>ko</u>pah

1 What food?

Name the numbered items.

❶ nuts
❷ seafood
❸ meat
❹ sugar
glass ❺

2 This is my...

1 **Ésta es mi mujer.**
   <u>es</u>tah es mee
   moo-<u>hair</u>

2 **Aquí están sus hijas.**
   ah<u>kee</u> es<u>tan</u> soos
   <u>ee</u>-has

3 **Su mesa es de no fumadores.**
   soo <u>me</u>sah es day
   noh fooma<u>do</u>res

2 This is my...

Say these phrases in Spanish.
Use **mi(-s)**, **tu(-us)** or **su(-s)**.

1 *This is my wife.*

2 *Here are her daughters.*

3 *Their table is non-smoking.*

3 I'd like...

1 **Quisiera un café.**
   kee<u>syai</u>rah oon
   ka<u>fay</u>

2 **Quisiera churros.**
   kee<u>syai</u>rah
   <u>choo</u>rros

2 **Quisiera azúcar.**
   kee<u>syai</u>rah
   ah-<u>thoo</u>kar

4 **Quisiera un café con leche.**
   kee<u>syai</u>rah oon
   ka<u>fay</u> kon <u>le</u>chay

3 I'd like...

Say "I'd like" the following:

❶ black coffee
churros ❷
sugar ❸
coffee with milk ❹

6 *pasta*

knife 7

8 *cheese*

beer 10

9 *napkin*

What food?

6 **la pasta**
lah pastah

7 **el cuchillo**
el koochee-yoh

8 **el queso**
el kesoh

9 **la servilleta**
lah serbee-yetah

10 **la cerveza**
lah thairbaythah

4 Restaurant

You arrive at a restaurant. Join in the conversation, replying in Spanish following the English prompts.

Buenas tardes señora, señor.
1 *Ask for a table for six.*

¿Fumadores o no fumadores?
2 *Say: nonsmoking.*

Síganme, por favor.
3 *Ask for the menu.*

¿Quiere la carta de vinos?
4 *Say: No. Sparkling water, please.*

Muy bien.
5 *Say you don't have a glass.*

4 Restaurant

1 **Buenas tardes, quisiera una mesa para seis.**
bwenas tardes, keesyairah oonah mesah parah seys

2 **No fumadores.**
noh foomadores

3 **La carta, por favor.**
lah kartah, por fabor

4 **No. Agua con gas, por favor.**
noh. ahgwah kon gas, por fabor

5 **No tengo copa.**
noh tengoh kopah

1 Warm up

Say "he is" and "they are." (pp.14–15)

Say "he is not" and "they are not." (pp.14–15)

What is Spanish for "the children"? (pp.10–11)

Los días y los meses
Days and months

In Spanish, days of the week (**los días de la semana**) and months (**los meses**) do not have capital letters. Notice that you use **en** with months: **en abril** (*in April*), but **el** or **los** with days: **el/los lunes** (*on Monday/Mondays*).

2 Words to remember: days of the week

Familiarize yourself with these words and test yourself using the flap.

lunes loones	*Monday*	
martes martes	*Tuesday*	
miércoles myairkoles	*Wednesday*	
jueves hwebes	*Thursday*	 **Nos reunimos mañana.** mos reh-ooneemos manyanah *We meet tomorrow.*
viernes byernes	*Friday*	
sábado sabadoh	*Saturday*	
domingo domeengoh	*Sunday*	
hoy oy	*today*	
mañana manyanah	*tomorrow*	 **Tengo una reserva para hoy.** tengoh oonah reserbah parah oy *I have a reservation for today.*
ayer ah-yair	*yesterday*	

3 Useful phrases: days

Learn these phrases and then test yourself using the flap.

La reunión no es el martes. lah reh-oonyon noh es el martes	*The meeting isn't on Tuesday.*	
Trabajo los domingos. traba-hoh los domeengos	*I work on Sundays.*	

4 Words to remember: months

Familiarize yourself with these words and test yourself using the flap.

Nuestro aniversario es en julio.
nwestroh aneebairsaree-oh es en hoolee-oh
Our anniversary is in July.

Navidad es en diciembre.
nabeedad es en deethyembray
Christmas is in December.

January	**enero**	ehneroh
February	**febrero**	febreroh
March	**marzo**	marthoh
April	**abril**	abreel
May	**mayo**	mah-yoh
June	**junio**	hoonee-oh
July	**julio**	hoolee-oh
August	**agosto**	agostoh
September	**septiembre**	septyembray
October	**octubre**	oktoobray
November	**noviembre**	nobyembray
December	**diciembre**	deethyembray
month	**el mes**	el mes
year	**el año**	el anyoh

5 Useful phrases: months

Learn these phrases and then test yourself using the flap.

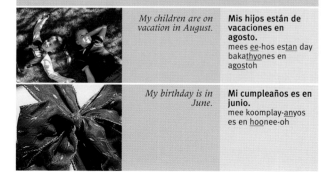

My children are on vacation in August.	**Mis hijos están de vacaciones en agosto.**	mees ee-hos estan day bakathyones en agostoh
My birthday is in June.	**Mi cumpleaños es en junio.**	mee koomplay-anyos es en hoonee-oh

La hora y los números
Time and numbers

The hour is preceded by **la** as in **la una** (*one o'clock*) and **las** for other numbers: **las dos**, **las tres**, and so on. In English the minutes sometimes come first (*"ten to five"*); in Spanish the hour comes first: **las cinco menos diez** (*"five minus ten"*).

2 Words to remember: time

Memorize how to tell the time in Spanish.

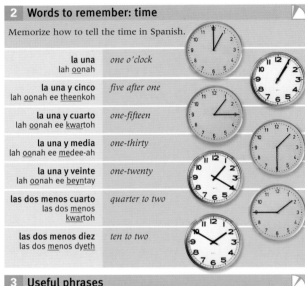

la una lah <u>oo</u>nah	*one o'clock*
la una y cinco lah <u>oo</u>nah ee <u>theen</u>koh	*five after one*
la una y cuarto lah <u>oo</u>nah ee <u>kwar</u>toh	*one-fifteen*
la una y media lah <u>oo</u>nah ee <u>me</u>dee-ah	*one-thirty*
la una y veinte lah <u>oo</u>nah ee <u>beyn</u>tay	*one-twenty*
las dos menos cuarto las dos <u>me</u>nos <u>kwar</u>toh	*quarter to two*
las dos menos diez las dos <u>me</u>nos d<u>yeth</u>	*ten to two*

3 Useful phrases

Learn these phrases and then test yourself using the cover flap.

¿Qué hora es? kay <u>o</u>rah es	*What time is it?*
¿A qué hora quiere el desayuno? ah kay <u>o</u>rah k<u>ya</u>iray el desah-<u>yoo</u>noh	*What time do you want breakfast?*
La reunión es a mediodía. lah reh-oon<u>yon</u> es ah maydyo<u>dee</u>-ah	*The meeting is at noon.*

4 Words to remember: higher numbers

To say 21 you use veinti and add **uno** (*one*): **veintiuno**. Successive numbers are created in the same way—for example, **veintidós** (22), **veintitrés** (23), and so on. After 30, link the numbers with **y** (*and*): **treinta y uno** (31), **cuarenta y cinco** (45), **sesenta y seis** (66).

Note the special forms used for 500, 700, and 900: **quinientos**, **setecientos**, and **novecientos**.

Quiero el autobús cincuenta y tres.
kyairoh el aootoboos theenkwentah ee tres
I want the route 53 bus.

eleven	**once** onthay
twelve	**doce** dothay
thirteen	**trece** trethay
fourteen	**catorce** katorthay
fifteen	**quince** keenthay
sixteen	**dieciséis** deeaytheeseyees
seventeen	**diecisiete** deeaytheesyeytay
eighteen	**dieciocho** deeaythyochoh
nineteen	**diecinueve** deeaythynwebay
twenty	**veinte** beyntay
thirty	**treinta** treyntah
forty	**cuarenta** kwarentah
fifty	**cincuenta** theenkwentah
sixty	**sesenta** sesentah
seventy	**setenta** setentah
eighty	**ochenta** ochentah
ninety	**noventa** nobentah
one hundred	**cien** theeayn
two hundred	**doscientos** dos-theeayntos
five hundred	**quinientos** keeneeayntos
one thousand	**mil** meel
two thousand	**dos mil** dos meel
one million	**un millón** oon mee-yon

5 Say it

25

68

84

91

five to ten.

eleven-thirty.

What time is lunch?

1 Warm up

Say the days of the week. (pp.28–9)

Say "three o'clock." (pp.30–1)

What's the Spanish for "today," "tomorrow," and "yesterday"? (pp.28–9)

Las citas
Appointments

Business in Spain is generally conducted more formally than in the United States. The Spanish also tend to leave the office for the lunch hour, often having a sit-down meal. Remember to use the formal forms of "you" (**usted**, **ustedes**) in business situations.

2 Useful phrases

Learn these phrases and then test yourself.

¿Nos reunimos mañana? nos reh-ooneemos manyanah	*Shall we meet tomorrow?*
¿Con quién? kon kee-en	*With whom?*
¿Cuándo está libre? kwandoh esta leebray	*When are you free?*
Lo siento, estoy ocupado(-a). loh syentoh, estoy okoopadoh(-ah)	*I'm sorry, I'm busy.*
¿Qué tal el jueves? keh tal el hwebes	*How about Thursday?*
A mí me va bien. ah mee may bah byen	*That's good for me.*

el apretón de manos
 el apreton day manos
 handshake

Bienvenido.
 byenveneedoh
 Welcome.

3 In conversation

Buenos días. Tengo una cita.
 bwenos deeyas. tengoh oonah theetah

Good morning. I have an appointment.

¿Con quién es la cita?
 kon kee-en es lah theetah

With whom is the appointment?

Con el Señor Montoya.
 kon el senyor montoyah

With Mr. Montoya.

4 Put into practice

Join in this conversation. Read the Spanish beside the pictures on the left and then follow the instructions to make your reply. Then test yourself by concealing the answers on the right with the cover flap.

¿Nos reunimos el jueves?
nos reh-ooneemos el hwebes?
Shall we meet Thursday?

Say: Sorry, I'm busy.

Lo siento, estoy ocupado(-a).
loh syentoh, estoy okoopadoh(-ah)

¿Cuándo está libre?
kwandoh esta leebray
When are you free?

Say: Tuesday afternoon.

El martes por la tarde.
el martes por lah tarday

A mí me va bien.
ah mee may bah byen
That's good for me.

Ask: At what time?

¿A qué hora?
ah kay orah

A las cuatro, si a usted le va bien.
ah las kwatroh, see ah oosted le bah byen
At four o'clock, if that's good for you.

Say: Yes, it's good for me.

Sí, me va bien.
see, may bah byen

Muy bien. ¿A qué hora?
mwee byen. ah kay orah?

Okay. What time?

A las tres, pero llego un poco tarde.
ah las tres, peroh yegoh oon pokoh tarday

At three o'clock, but I'm a little late.

No se preocupe. Tome asiento, por favor.
noh say pre-ohkoopay. tomay asyaintoh, por fabor

Don't worry. Take a seat, please.

Say "I'm sorry."
(pp.32–3)

What is the Spanish
for "I'd like an
appointment"?
(pp.32–3)

How do you say
"when?" in Spanish?
(pp.32–3)

Por teléfono
On the telephone

The emergency number for police,
ambulance, or fire services is 112.
For directory assistance, dial 11818.
Telephone cards can be used with
public or private phones by dialing in
a code. Available from newsstands and
tobacconists, they are a cheap way to
call overseas.

2 Match and repeat

Match the numbered items to the Spanish
in the panel on the left, then test yourself.

1 **el cargador**
   el kargador

2 **el contestador
   automático**
   el kontestador
   aootomateekoh

3 **la tarjeta
   telefónica**
   lah tarhetah
   telefoneekah

4 **el móvil**
   el mobeel

5 **los auriculares**
   los aooreekoolares

charger ❶

cell phone ❹

headphones ❺   *phone card* ❸

3 In conversation

**Dígame, Susana
Castillo al habla.**
deegamay, soosanah
kasteeyoh al ablah

*Hello. Susana Castillo
speaking.*

**Buenos días. Quisiera
hablar con Julián
López, por favor.**
bwenos deeyas.
keesyair-ah ablar kon
hooleean lopeth, por
fabor

*Hello. I'd like to speak
to Julián López, please.*

¿De parte de quién?
day partay day kee-en?

Who's calling?

4 Useful phrases

Practice these phrases and then test yourself using the cover flap.

I'd like an outside line.

Quisiera una línea externa.
kee<u>syai</u>rah <u>oo</u>nah <u>lee</u>neah ex<u>ter</u>nah

---

Quiero llamar a cobro revertido.
<u>kye</u>roh y<u>amar</u> ah <u>ko</u>broh rreber<u>tee</u>doh
I'd like to make a collect call.

I'd like to speak to María Alfaro.

Quisiera hablar con María Alfaro.
kee<u>syai</u>rah a<u>blar</u> kon mar<u>eeah</u> al<u>fa</u>roh

---

2 *answering machine*

Can I leave a message?

¿Puedo dejar un mensaje?
<u>pwe</u>doh de<u>har</u> oon men<u>sa</u>hay

---

5 Say it

I'd like to speak to Mr. Girona.

Can I leave a message for Antonio?

Sorry, I have the wrong number.

Perdone, me he equivocado de número.
per<u>do</u>nay, may ay ekeebo<u>ka</u>doh day <u>noo</u>meroh

---

José Ortega, de Imprentas Lacuesta.
ho<u>say</u> or<u>te</u>gah, day eem<u>pren</u>tas la<u>kwes</u>tah

José Ortega of Lacuesta Printers.

Lo siento. La línea está comunicando.
loh <u>syain</u>toh. lah <u>lee</u>neah es<u>tah</u> komoonee<u>kan</u>doh

I'm sorry. The line is busy.

¿Le puede decir que me llame, por favor?
lay <u>pwe</u>day de<u>theer</u> kay may <u>ya</u>may, por fa<u>bor</u>

Can you ask him to call me, please?

Repase y repita
Review and repeat

1 Sums

1 **dieciséis**
   deeaythee<u>say</u>ees

2 **treinta y nueve**
   <u>treyn</u>tah ee
   <u>nwe</u>bay

3 **cincuenta y tres**
   theen<u>kwen</u>tah ee
   tres

4 **setenta y cuatro**
   se<u>ten</u>tah ee
   <u>kwa</u>troh

5 **noventa y nueve**
   no<u>ben</u>tah ee
   <u>nwe</u>bay

1 Sums

Say the answers
to these sums out
loud in Spanish.
Then check to see
if you remembered
correctly.

1 $10 + 6 = ?$

2 $14 + 25 = ?$

3 $66 - 13 = ?$

4 $40 + 34 = ?$

5 $90 + 9 = ?$

3 Telephones

What are the numbered
items in Spanish?

cell phone ❶

phone card ❸

2 I want...

1 **Quiere**
   <u>kyai</u>ray

2 **quiere**
   <u>kyai</u>ray

3 **queremos**
   ke<u>ray</u>mos

4 **quieres**
   <u>kyai</u>res

5 **quieren**
   <u>kyai</u>ren

6 **quiero**
   <u>kyai</u>roh

2 I want...

Fill in the blanks
with the correct
form of **querer** (*to
want*).

1 ¿ _____ usted un
   café?

2 **Ella** _____ **ir de
   vacaciones.**

3 **Nosotros** _____ **una mesa para tres.**

4 **Tú** _____ **una cerveza.**

5 **Ellos** _____ **una mesa para dos.**

6 **Yo** _____ **caramelos.**

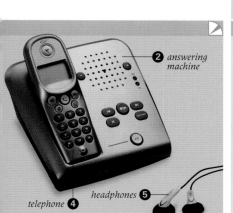

2 *answering machine*

telephone 4   *headphones* 5

3   Telephones

1   **el móvil**
el <u>mo</u>beel

2   **el contestador automático**
el kontesta<u>dor</u> aooto<u>ma</u>teekoh

3   **la tarjeta telefónica**
lah tar<u>he</u>tah tele<u>fo</u>neekah

4   **el teléfono**
el te<u>le</u>fonoh

5   **los auriculares**
los aooreekoo<u>la</u>res

4   When?

What do these sentences mean?

1   **Tengo una cita el lunes veinte de mayo.**

2   **Mi cumpleaños es en septiembre.**

3   **Hoy es domingo.**

4   **No trabajo en agosto.**

4   When?

1   *I have a meeting on Monday, May 20th.*

2   *My birthday is in September.*

3   *Today is Sunday.*

4   *I don't work in August.*

5   Time

Say these times in Spanish.

5   Time

1   **la una**
lah <u>oo</u>nah

2   **la una y cinco**
la <u>oo</u>nah ee <u>theen</u>koh

3   **la una y veinte**
lah <u>oo</u>nah ee <u>beyn</u>tay

4   **la una y media**
lah <u>oo</u>nah ee <u>me</u>dee-ah

5   **la una y cuarto**
lah <u>oo</u>nah ee <u>kwar</u>toh

6   **las dos menos diez**
las dos <u>me</u>nos dyeth

1 Warm up

Count to 100 in tens.
(pp.10–11, pp.30–1)

Ask "What time is it?"
(pp.30–1)

Say "One-thirty."
(pp.30–1)

En la oficina de billetes
At the ticket office

In Spain, commuter trains are very economical, clean, and efficient. Long-distance trains still offer smoking and nonsmoking carriages, and the prices vary depending on what day you travel, blue days being the cheapest.

2 Words to remember

Learn these words and then test yourself.

la estación lah estath<u>yon</u>	*(train) station*
la terminal lah termee<u>nal</u>	*(bus) station*
el billete el bee<u>ye</u>tay	*ticket*
de ida day <u>ee</u>dah	*one-way*
de ida y vuelta day <u>ee</u>dah ee <u>bwel</u>tah	*round-trip*
de primera day preem<u>e</u>rah	*first class*
de segunda day seg<u>oon</u>dah	*second class*
el descuento el des<u>kwen</u>toh	*discount*

el pasajero
el pasa<u>hai</u>roh
passenger

la señal
lah sen<u>yal</u>
sign

La estación está llena de gente.
lah estath<u>yon</u> est<u>ah</u>
<u>ye</u>nah day <u>hen</u>tay
The station is crowded.

3 In conversation

Dos billetes para Bilbao, por favor.
dos bee<u>ye</u>tes <u>pa</u>rah
bee<u>ba</u>-oh, por fa<u>bor</u>

Two tickets to Bilbao, please.

¿De ida y vuelta?
day <u>ee</u>dah y <u>bwel</u>tah

Round-trip?

Si. ¿Necesito reservar asiento?
see. nethe<u>see</u>toh
rreseer<u>bar</u> as<u>yain</u>toh

Yes. Do I need to reserve seats?

4 Useful phrases

Learn these phrases and then test yourself using the cover flap.

Mi tren va con retraso.
mee tren bah kon
rretrasoh
My train is late.

el tren   **el andén**
el tren   el anden
train   *platform*

How much is a ticket to Madrid?	**¿Cuánto cuesta un billete para Madrid?** kwantoh kwaystah oon beeyetay parah madreed
Can I pay by credit card?	**¿Puedo pagar con tarjeta de crédito?** pwedoh pagar kon tarhetah day kredeetoh
Do I have to change trains?	**¿Tengo que cambiar?** tengoh kay kambee-ar
Which platform does the train leave from?	**¿De qué andén sale el tren?** day kay anden salay el tren
Are there any discounts?	**¿Hay algún descuento?** ah-ee algoon deskwentoh
What time does the train to Gijón leave?	**¿A qué hora sale el tren para Gijón?** ah kay orah salay el tren parah geehon

5 Say it

Which platform does the train to Madrid leave from?

Three round-trip tickets to Murcia, please.

Cultural tip

Most train stations now have automatic ticket machines that will often also take credit cards.

No hace falta. Cuarenta euros, por favor.
noh ahthay faltah.
kwarentah eh-ooros, por
fabor

That's not necessary. Forty euros, please.

¿Aceptan tarjetas de crédito?
ahtheptan tarhetas day kredeetoh

Do you take credit cards?

Si. El tren sale del andén cinco.
see. el tren salay del anden theenkoh

Yes. The train leaves from platform five.

1 Warm up

What is "train" in Spanish? (pp.38–9)

What does "¿De qué andén sale el tren?" mean? (pp.38–9)

Ask "When are you free?" (pp.32–3)

Ir y coger
To go and to take

The verbs **ir** (*to go*) and **coger** (*to take*) allow you to create many useful sentences. Note that **coger** can also mean to catch: **coger una pelota** (*to catch a ball*), **coger un resfriado** (*to catch a cold*); to grab: **coger a alguien** (*to grab someone*); and to hold: **coger a un bebé** (*to hold a baby*).

2 Ir: to go

Spanish uses the same form of **ir** for both *I go* and *I am going*: **voy a Madrid** (*I am going to Madrid/I go to Madrid*). The same is true of other verbs—for example, **cojo el metro** (*I am taking the metro/I take the metro*).

yo voy yoh boy	*I go*
tú vas/usted va too bas/oosted bah	*you go (informal/ formal singular)*
él/ella va el/eh-yah bah	*he/she goes*
nosotros(-as) vamos nosotros(-as) bamos	*we go*
vosotros(-as) vais/ ustedes van bosotros/-as baees/ oostedes ban	*you go (informal/ formal plural)*
ellos/ellas van eh-yos/eh-yas ban	*they go*
¿A dónde vas? ah donday bas	*Where are you going?*
Voy a Madrid. boy ah madreed	*I am going to Madrid.*

Voy a la Plaza de España.
boy ah lah plathah day espanyah
I am going to the Plaza de España.

Conversational tip You may have noticed that "de" (of) combines with "el" to produce "del" as in "Museo del Prado" (literally, museum of the Prado); "el menú del día" (menu of the day). In the same way, "a" (to) combines with "el" to produce "al": "Voy al museo" (I'm going to the museum). With feminine and plural words, "de" remains separate from "la," "los," and "las."

3 Coger: to take

Say the present tense of **coger** (*to take*) aloud. Use the cover flap to test yourself. When you are confident, practice the sentences below.

yo cojo yoh <u>ko</u>hoh	*I take*
tú coges/usted coge too <u>ko</u>hes/oo<u>sted</u> <u>ko</u>hay	*you take (informal/ formal singular)*
él/ella coge el/<u>eh</u>-yah <u>ko</u>hay	*he/she takes*
nosotros(-as) cogemos no<u>so</u>tros(-as) ko<u>hay</u>mos	*we take*
vosotros(-as) cogéis/ustedes cogen bo<u>so</u>tros(-as) kohe-<u>ees</u>/ oo<u>sted</u>es <u>ko</u>hen	*you take (informal/ formal plural)*
ellos/ellas cogen <u>eh</u>-yos/<u>eh</u>-yas <u>ko</u>hen	*they take*

Yo cojo el metro todos los días.
yoh <u>ko</u>hoh el <u>me</u>troh <u>to</u>dos los <u>dee</u>yas
I take the metro every day.

No quiero coger un taxi. noh <u>kyai</u>roh ko<u>her</u> oon <u>tak</u>see	*I don't want to take a taxi.*

Coja la primera a la izquierda. <u>ko</u>hah lah pree<u>mer</u>ah ah lah eeth<u>kyair</u>dah	*Take the first left.*

4 Put into practice

Cover the text on the right and complete the dialogue in Spanish.

¿A dónde va? ah <u>don</u>day bah *Where are you going?* Say: I'm going to the Puerta del Sol.	**Voy a la Puerta del Sol.** boy ah lah <u>pwer</u>tah del sol

¿Quiere coger el autobús? <u>kyai</u>ray ko<u>her</u> el aooto<u>boos</u> *Do you want to take the bus?* Say: No, I want to go by metro.	**No, quiero ir en metro.** noh, <u>kyai</u>roh eer en <u>me</u>troh

Taxi, autobús, y metro
Taxi, bus, and metro

The metro and some buses operate a ticket system where you have to validate your tickets in a machine. There's a standard fare per ride, but you can also buy a **metrobús**, a book of 10 tickets for both buses and metro.

2 Words to remember

Familiarize yourself with these words.

el autobús el aooto<u>boos</u>	*bus*
la taquilla lah ta<u>kee</u>yah	*ticket office*
la estación de metro lah estath<u>yon</u> day <u>me</u>troh	*metro station*
la parada de autobús lah pa<u>ra</u>dah day aooto<u>boos</u>	*bus stop*
la tarifa lah ta<u>ree</u>fah	*fare*
el taxi el <u>tak</u>see	*taxi*
la parada de taxis lah pa<u>ra</u>dah day <u>tak</u>sees	*taxi stand*

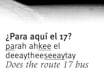

¿Para aquí el 17?
<u>pa</u>rah ah<u>kee</u> el deeaythee<u>seeay</u>tay
Does the route 17 bus stop here?

3 In conversation: taxi

A la Plaza de España, por favor.
ah lah <u>pla</u>thah day es<u>pa</u>nyah, por fa<u>bor</u>

Plaza de España, please.

Sí, de acuerdo, señor.
see, day a<u>kwair</u>do, sen<u>yor</u>

Yes, certainly, sir.

¿Me puede dejar aquí, por favor?
may <u>pwe</u>day de<u>har</u> ah<u>kee</u>, por fa<u>bor</u>

Can you drop me here, please?

4 Useful phrases

Practice these phrases and then test yourself using the cover flap.

I'd like a taxi to go to the Prado.

Quisiera un taxi para ir al Prado.
keesyairah oon taksee parah eer al prado

When is the next bus?

¿Cuándo sale el próximo autobús?
kwandoh salay el prokseemoh aootoboos

How do you get to the museum?

¿Cómo se va al museo?
komoh say bah al moosayoh

How long is the trip?

¿Cuánto dura el viaje?
kwantoh doorah el beeahay

Please wait for me.

Espéreme, por favor.
esperemay, por fabor

Cultural tip Metro lines in Madrid are known by numbers and the names of the first and last stations. Look for the relevant end station. The Madrid metro runs every day between 6:00 am and 2:00 am.

6 Say it

Do you go near the train station?

Do you go near the Prado?

When's the next bus to Barcelona?

5 In conversation: bus

¿Pasa cerca del museo?
pasah therkah del moosayoh

Do you go near the museum?

Sí. Son 80 céntimos.
see. son ochentah thenteemos

Yes. That's 80 cents.

Avíseme cuando lleguemos.
abeesemay kwandoh yeghemos

Tell me when we arrive.

En la carretera
On the road

1 Warm up

How do you say "I have..."? (pp.14–15)

Say "my father," "my sister," and "my parents." (pp.10–11, pp.12–13)

Say "I'm going to Madrid." (pp.40–1)

Spanish **autopistas** (*toll highways*) are fast but can be quite expensive. You will find signs for **el peaje** (*toll payment stations*). These have multiple lanes. Make sure you enter a green lane that allows payment by cash or credit card. Some lanes are for pass-holders or trucks only.

2 Match and repeat

Match the numbered items to the list on the left, then test yourself.

1 **el maletero**
   el malaytairoh

2 **el parabrisas**
   el parabreesas

3 **el capó**
   el kapoh

4 **la rueda**
   lah rwedah

5 **el neumático**
   el ne-oomateekoh

6 **la puerta**
   lah pwertah

7 **los faros**
   los faros

8 **el parachoques**
   el parachokes

Cultural tip Some self-service gas stations can be unattended. In this case, you usually have to specify how many liters you want and pay by card *before* filling up.

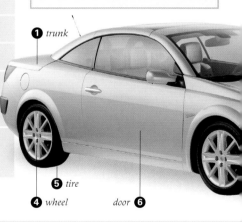

❶ *trunk*

❺ *tire*

❹ *wheel*   *door* ❻

3 Road features

la rotonda
lah rrotonduh

roundabout

el semáforo
el semaforoh

traffic lights

el cruce
el kroothay

intersection

4 Useful phrases

Learn these phrases and then test yourself using the cover flap.

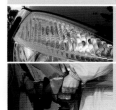

	The turn signal doesn't work.	**El intermitente no funciona.**
		el intairmee<u>tain</u>tay noh foon<u>thyon</u>ah
	Fill it up, please.	**Lleno, por favor.**
		<u>yen</u>noh, por fa<u>bor</u>

5 Words to remember

Familiarize yourself with these words, then test yourself using the flap.

6 Say it

There's something wrong with my engine.

I have a flat tire.

2 *windshield*

3 *hood*

7 *headlights*   *bumper* **8**

gasoline	**la gasolina** lah gaso<u>lee</u>nah
diesel	**el gasoil** el ga<u>soil</u>
oil	**el aceite** el ah-tha<u>yee</u>tay
engine	**el motor** el mo<u>tor</u>
gearbox	**la caja de cambios** lah <u>ka</u>hah day <u>kam</u>byos
turn signal	**el intermitente** el intairmee<u>tain</u>tay
flat tire	**la rueda pinchada** lah <u>rway</u>dah peen<u>cha</u>dah
exhaust	**el tubo de escape** el <u>too</u>boh day es<u>ka</u>pay
driver's license	**el carné de conducir** el kar<u>nay</u> day kondoo<u>theer</u>

la autopista
lah aooto<u>pees</u>tah

highway/expressway

la autopista de peaje
lah aooto<u>pees</u>tah day <u>pya</u>hay

toll highway

el atasco de tráfico
el a<u>tas</u>koh day <u>tra</u>feekoh

traffic jam

Respuestas
Answers
Cover with flap

Repase y repita
Review and repeat

1 Transportation

1 **el autobús**
el aooto<u>boos</u>

2 **el taxi**
el <u>tak</u>see

3 **el coche**
el <u>ko</u>chay

4 **la bicicleta**
lah beethee<u>kle</u>tah

5 **el metro**
el <u>me</u>troh

1 Transportation

Name these forms of transport in Spanish.

bus ❶

metro ❺

2 Go and take

1 **ir**
eer

2 **cojo**
<u>ko</u>hoh

3 **va**
bah

4 **vamos**
<u>ba</u>mos

5 **cogen**
<u>ko</u>hen

6 **voy**
boy

2 Go and take

Use the correct form of the verb in brackets.

1 Quiero _____ a la estación. (ir)

2 Yo _____ el metro. (coger)

3 ¿A dónde _____ usted? (ir)

4 Nosotros _____ al Museo
del Prado. (ir)

5 Ellos _____ (coger)
un taxi.

6 Yo _____ (ir) a Madrid.

2 taxi

3 car

4 bicycle

3 You?

Use the correct form for **usted** or **tú** in each sentence.

1 *You are in a café. Ask "Do you have churros?"*

2 *You are with a friend. Ask "Do you want a beer?"*

3 *A visitor approaches you at your company's reception desk. Ask "Do you have an ppointment?"*

4 *You are on the bus. Ask "Do you go near the station?"*

5 *Ask your friend where she's going tomorrow.*

3 You?

1 **¿Tiene churros?**
tyenay choorros

2 **¿Quieres una cerveza?**
kyaires oonah thairbaythah

3 **¿Tiene una cita?**
tyenay oonah theetah

4 **¿Pasa cerca de la estación?**
pasah therkah day lah estathyon

5 **¿A dónde vas mañana?**
ah donday bas manyanah

4 Tickets

You're buying tickets at a train station. Follow the conversation, replying in Spanish following the numbered English prompts.

¿Qué desea?
1 *I'd like two tickets to Sevilla.*

¿De ida o de ida y vuelta?
2 *Round-trip, please.*

Muy bien. Cincuenta euros, por favor.
3 *What time does the train leave?*

A las tres y diez.
4 *What platform does the train leave from?*

Andén número siete.
5 *Thank you very much. Goodbye.*

4 Tickets

1 **Quisiera dos billetes para Sevilla.**
keesyairah dos beeyetes parah sebeeyah

2 **De ida y vuelta, por favor.**
day eedah ee bweltah, por fabor

3 **¿A qué hora sale el tren?**
ah kay orah salay el tren

4 **¿De qué andén sale el tren?**
day kay anden salay el tren

5 **Muchas gracias. Adiós.**
moochas grathyas. addy-os

1 Warm up

Ask "How do you get to the museum?" (pp.42–3)

Say "I want to take the metro" and "I don't want to take a taxi." (pp.40–1)

En la ciudad
Around town

Note that the Spanish word **museo** (*museum*) also means art gallery when it's a public building in which works of art are exhibited; **galería de arte** usually refers to a shop that sells works of art. Be careful, too, not to confuse **librería** (*bookshop* or *bookshelf*) and **biblioteca** (*library*).

2 Match and repeat

Match the numbered locations to the words in the panel.

1 **el ayuntamiento**
   el ahyoonta-myaintoh

2 **el puente**
   el pwentay

3 **el centro**
   el thentroh

4 **la iglesia**
   lah eegleseeah

5 **la plaza**
   lah plathah

6 **el aparcamiento**
   el aparka-myaintoh

7 **la biblioteca**
   lah bibleeotekah

8 **el museo**
   el moosayoh

❶ town hall

church ❹

downtown ❸

❷ bridge

❺ *square*

3 Words to remember

Familiarize yourself with these words and test yourself using the cover flap.

la gasolinera lah gasoleenerah	*gas station*
la oficina de información turística lah ohfeetheenah day eenformathyon tooreesteekah	*tourist information*
la piscina municipal lah pistheenah mooneetheepal	*public swimming pool*

❼ *library*

Conversational tip In Spanish there are two ways of saying "am," "is," or "are." You have already learned the verb "ser" (p.14): "soy inglés" (I am English); "es vegetariano" (he is vegetarian). When talking about where something is, you need to use a different verb: "estar." The most important forms of this verb are: "estoy" (I am), "está" (he/she/it is), and "están" (they are): "¿Dónde están lla iglesia?" (Where is the church?); "El café no está lejos." (The café isn't far.)

4 Useful phrases

Practice these phrases and then test yourself using the cover flap.

Is there an art gallery in town?	**¿Hay alguna museo de arte en la ciudad?** ah-ee algoonah moosayoh day artay en lah thyoodad
Is it far from here?	**¿Está lejos de aquí?** estah lehos day ahkee
There is a swimming pool near the bridge.	**Hay una piscina cerca del puente.** ah-ee oonah peestheenah therkah del pwentay

La catedral está en el centro.
lah katedral estah en el thentroh
The cathedral is downtown.

5 Put into practice

Join in this conversation. Read the Spanish on the left and follow the instructions to make your reply. Then test yourself.

¿Le puedo ayudar? lay pwedoh ahyoodar *Can I help you?* Ask: *Is there a library in town?*	**¿Hay alguna biblioteca en la ciudad?** ah-ee algoonah beeblyotekah en lah thyoodad
No, pero hay un museo. noh, peroh ah-ee oon moosayoh *No, but there's a museum.* Ask: *How do I get to the museum?*	**¿Cómo se va al museo?** komoh say bah al moosayoh
Está por allí. estah por ahyee *It's over there.* Say: *Thank you very much.*	**Muchas gracias.** moochas grathyas

 6 *parking lot*

8 *museum*

Las direcciones
Directions

1 Warm up

How do you say "near the station"? (pp.42–3)

Say "Take the first left." (pp.40–1)

Ask "Where are you going?" (pp.40–1)

You'll often be able to find a **plano de la ciudad** (*town map*) in the downtown area, usually near the town hall or tourist office. In the older parts of Spanish towns there are often narrow streets, in which you will usually find a one-way system in operation. Parking is usually restricted.

el bloque de oficinas
el blokay day ohfeetheenas
office block

2 Useful phrases

Learn these phrases and then test yourself.

Tuerza a la izquierda/derecha. twerthah ah lah eethkyairdah/ derechah	*Turn left/right.*
Todo recto. todoh rrektoh	*Straight on.*
¿Cómo se va a la piscina? komoh say bah ah lah peestheenah	*How do I get to the swimming pool?*
la primera a la derecha lah preemerah ah lah derechah	*first right*
la segunda a la izquierda lah segoondah ah lah eethkyairdah	*second left*

la fuente
lah fwentay
fountain

3 In conversation

¿Hay un restaurante en la ciudad?
ah-ee oon restaoorantay en la thyoodad

Is there a restaurant in town?

Sí, cerca de la estación.
see, therkah day lah estathyon

Yes, near the station.

¿Cómo se va a la estación?
komoh say bah ah lah estathyon

How do I get to the station?

4 Words to remember

Familiarize yourself with these words and test yourself using the flap.

Me he perdido.
may eh per<u>dee</u>doh
I'm lost.

el centro deportivo
el <u>then</u>troh
depor<u>tee</u>boh
gym

traffic lights	**el semáforo** el se<u>ma</u>foroh
corner	**la esquina** lah es<u>kee</u>nah
street/road	**la calle** lah <u>kayay</u>
main road	**la calle principal** lah <u>kayay</u> preen<u>thee</u>pal
at the end of the street	**al final de la calle** al fee<u>nal</u> day lah <u>kayay</u>
map	**el plano** el <u>plano</u>h
overpass	**el paso elevado** el <u>pa</u>soh ele<u>ba</u>doh
across from	**enfrente de** en<u>fren</u>tay day

la zona peatonal
lah <u>tho</u>nah
pe-ah<u>to</u>nal
pedestrian zone

¿Dondé estamos?
<u>don</u>day es<u>ta</u>mos
Where are we?

5 Say it

Turn right at the end of the street.

Turn left across from the museum.

It's ten minutes by bus.

Tuerza a la izquierda en el semáforo.
<u>twer</u>thah ah lah eeth<u>kyair</u>dah en el se<u>ma</u>foroh

Turn left at the traffic lights.

¿Está lejos?
es<u>tah</u> <u>le</u>hos

Is it far?

No, cinco minutos andando.
noh, <u>theen</u>koh
mee<u>noo</u>tos an<u>dan</u>doh

No, it's five minutes on foot.

1 Warm up

Say the days of the week in Spanish. (pp.28–9)

How do you say "six o'clock"? (pp.30–1)

Ask "What time is it?" (pp.30–1)

El turismo
Sightseeing

Most national museums and art galleries close on Mondays and public holidays. Although stores are normally closed on Sundays, many will open in tourist areas. It is not unusual for public buildings and shops to close at lunchtime, between 1:30 and 4:30 pm.

2 Words to remember

Familiarize yourself with these words and test yourself using the flap.

la guía lah *gheeah*	*guidebook*
la entrada lah en*tra*dah	*admission ticket*
el horario de apertura el o*rar*yoh day apertoorah	*opening times*
el día festivo el *dee*yah fes*tee*voh	*public holiday*
entrada libre en*tra*dah *lee*bray	*free admission*

la visita con guía
 lah bee*see*tah kon *ghee*ah
 guided tour

> **Cultural tip** If a public holiday falls on a Thursday or a Tuesday, the Spanish will often "hacer puente" (do a bridge)—in other words, take Friday or Monday off to make a long weekend.

3 In conversation

¿Abren esta tarde?
 *ah*bren es*tah *tar*day

Are you open this afternoon?

Sí, pero cerramos a las cuatro.
 see, *peroh* ther*ra*mos ah las *kwa*troh

Yes, but we close at four o'clock.

¿Tienen acceso para sillas de ruedas?
 *tye*nen ak*the*soh *pa*rah *see*yas day *rwe*das

Do you have access for wheelchairs?

4 Useful phrases

Practice these phrases and then test yourself using the cover flap.

What time do you open/close?

¿A qué hora abre/cierra?
ah kay orah ahbray/thyairrah

Where are the restrooms?

¿Dónde están los servicios?
donday estan los serbeethyos

Is there access for wheelchairs?

¿Hay acceso para sillas de ruedas?
ah-ee akthesoh parah seeyas day rwedas

5 Put into practice

Cover the text on the right and complete the dialogue in Spanish.

Lo siento, el museo está cerrado.
loh syentoh, el moosayoh estah therradoh
Sorry. The museum is closed.

Ask: Are you open on Tuesdays?

¿Abren los martes?
ahbren los martes

Sí, pero cerramos temprano.
see, peroh therramos tempranoh
Yes, but we close early.

Ask: At what time?

¿A qué hora?
ah kay orah

Sí, el ascensor está allí.
see, el asthensor estah ah-yee

Yes, there's an elevator over there.

Gracias, quisiera cuatro entradas.
grathyas, keesyairah kwatroh entradas

Thank you, I'd like four admission tickets.

Aquí tiene, y la guía es gratis.
ahkee tyenay, ee lah gheeah es gratees

Here you are, and the guidebook is free.

En el aeropuerto
At the airport

1 Warm up

Say "one-thirty."
(pp.30–1)

What's the Spanish for
"ticket"? (pp.38–9)

Say "I am going to
New York." (pp.40–1)

Although the airport environment is
largely international, it is sometimes
useful to be able to ask your way
around the terminal in Spanish. It's a
good idea to make sure you have a
few coins when you arrive at the
airport; you may need to pay for a
luggage cart.

2 Words to remember

Familiarize yourself with these words and test yourself using the flap.

la facturación lah faktoorath<u>yon</u>	*check-in*
las salidas las sal<u>ee</u>das	*departures*
las llegadas las yeh<u>ga</u>das	*arrivals*
la aduana lah <u>adwa</u>nah	*customs*
el control de pasaportes el kon<u>trol</u> day pasa<u>por</u>tes	*passport control*
la terminal lah termee<u>nal</u>	*terminal*
la puerta de embarque lah <u>pwer</u>tah day em<u>bar</u>kay	*boarding gate*

**¿Cuál es la puerta de
embarque para el
vuelo veintitrés?**
kwal es lah <u>pwer</u>tah day
em<u>bar</u>kay <u>pa</u>rah el
<u>bwe</u>loh bayeentee<u>tres</u>
*What is the boarding
gate for flight 23?*

3 Useful phrases

Learn these phrases and then test yourself using the cover flap.

¿Sale a su hora el vuelo para Sevilla? <u>sa</u>lay ah soo <u>o</u>rah el <u>bwe</u>loh <u>pa</u>rah se<u>vee</u>yah	*Is the flight to Seville on time?*

No encuentro mi equipaje. noh en<u>kwen</u>troh mee ehkee<u>pa</u>hay	*I can't find my luggage.*

4 Put into practice

Join in this conversation. Read the Spanish on the left and follow the instructions to make your reply. Then test yourself by concealing the answers using the cover flap.

Hola, ¿le puedo ayudar?
o-lah, lay pwedoh ahyoodar
Hello, can I help you?

Ask: Is the flight to Madrid on time?

¿Sale a su hora el vuelo para Madrid?
salay ah soo orah el bweloh parah madreed

Sí señor.
see senyor
Yes sir.

Ask: What is the boarding gate?

¿Cuál es la puerta de embarque?
kwal es lah pwertah day embarkay

← **i** Información

5 Match and repeat

Match the numbered items to the Spanish words in the panel.

boarding ❶ pass

check-in ❷ desk

ticket ❸

passport ❹

❺ suitcase ❻ carry-on luggage ❼ cart

1 **la tarjeta de embarque**
lah tarhetah day embarkay

2 **el mostrador de facturación**
el mostrador day faktoorathyon

3 **el billete**
el beeyehtay

4 **el pasaporte**
el pasaportay

5 **la maleta**
lah malaytah

6 **el equipaje de mano**
el ehkeepahay day manoh

7 **el carrito**
el karreetoh

Repase y repita
Review and repeat

1 Places

1 **el museo**
el moo<u>say</u>oh

2 **el ayuntamiento**
el ahyoonta-<u>myain</u>toh

3 **el puente**
el <u>pwen</u>tay

4 **la biblioteca**
lah beeblee-oh<u>tek</u>ah

5 **el aparcamiento**
el ahparka-<u>myain</u>toh

6 **la catedral**
lah kate<u>dral</u>

7 **la plaza**
lah <u>plath</u>ah

1 Places

Name the numbered places in Spanish.

 ❶ *museum*   ❷ *town hall*   ❸ *bridge*

 ❹ *library*   ❺ *parking lot* ❻ *cathedral*

❼ *square*

2 Car parts

1 **el parabrisas**
el para<u>bree</u>sas

2 **el intermitente**
el intairmee-<u>tain</u>tay

3 **el capó**
el ka<u>poh</u>

4 **el neumático**
el ne-ooma<u>tee</u>koh

5 **la puerta**
lah <u>pwer</u>tah

6 **el parachoques**
el para<u>cho</u>kes

2 Car parts

Name these car parts in Spanish.

windshield ❶

❹ *tire* ❺ *door*

3 Questions

Ask the questions that match these answers.

1 **El autobús sale a las ocho.**
el aooto<u>boos</u> <u>sal</u>ay ah las <u>o</u>choh

2 **El café es un euro cincuenta.**
el ka<u>fay</u> es oon eh-<u>oo</u>ro theen<u>kwen</u>tah

3 **No, no quiero vino.**
noh, noh <u>kyai</u>roh <u>bee</u>noh

4 **El tren sale del andén cinco.**
el tren <u>sal</u>ay del an<u>den</u> <u>theen</u>koh

5 **Nosotros vamos a León.**
no<u>sot</u>ros <u>ba</u>mos ah leh-<u>on</u>

6 **El próximo tren es dentro de quince minutos.**
el <u>prok</u>seemoh tren es <u>den</u>troh day <u>keen</u>thay <u>mee</u>nootos

3 Questions

1 **¿A qué hora sale el autobús?**
ah kay <u>orah</u> <u>sal</u>ay el aooto<u>boos</u>

2 **¿Cuánto es el café?**
<u>kwan</u>toh es el ka<u>fay</u>

3 **¿Quieres vino?**
<u>kyai</u>res <u>bee</u>noh

4 **¿De qué andén sale el tren?**
day kay an<u>den</u> <u>sal</u>ay el tren

5 **¿A dónde vais?**
ah <u>don</u>day baees

6 **¿Cuándo es el próximo tren?**
<u>kwan</u>doh es el <u>prok</u>seemoh tren

2 *turn signal*

3 *hood*

6 *bumper*

4 Verbs

Choose the correct form of the verb in brackets to fill in the blanks.

1 Yo ___ inglés. (ser)

2 Nosotros ___ el metro. (tomar)

3 Ella ___ a Marbella. (ir)

4 Él ___ casado. (estar)

5 ¿Tú ___ un té? (querer)

6 ¿Cuántos niños ___ usted? (tener)

4 Verbs

1 **soy**
soy

2 **cogemos**
ko<u>hay</u>mos

3 **va**
bah

4 **está**
es<u>tah</u>

5 **quieres**
<u>kyai</u>res

6 **tiene**
<u>tye</u>nay

1 Warm up

Ask "Do you accept credit cards?" (pp.38–9)

Ask "How much is that?" (pp.18–19)

Ask "Do you have children?" (pp.10–11)

Reservar una habitación
Booking a room

Types of accommodation in Spain include: **hotel**, categorized from one to five stars; **pensión**, a small family-run hotel; **hostal**, cheap and basic; and **parador**, state-owned hotels in historic properties or places of great beauty.

2 Useful phrases

Practice these phrases and then test yourself by concealing the Spanish on the left using the cover flap.

¿El desayuno está incluido?
el desa*yoo*noh es*tah* in*kloo*eedoh

Is breakfast included?

¿Aceptan animales de compañía?
a*thep*tan a*nee*males day kompan*yee*ah

Do you accept pets?

¿Tienen servicio de habitaciones?
t*yen*en ser*beeth*yoh day abeeta*thyo*nes

Do you have room service?

¿A qué hora tengo que dejar la habitación?
ah kay *orah tengoh* kay de*har* lah abeeta*thyon*

What time do I have to check out?

3 In conversation

¿Tiene habitaciones libres?
t*yenay* abeeta*thyo*nes *lee*bres

Do you have any vacancies?

Sí, una habitación doble.
see, *oo*nah abeeta*thyon doblay*

Yes, a double room.

¿Tiene una cuna?
t*yenay oo*nah *koo*nah

Do you have a crib?

4 Words to remember

Familiarize yourself with these words and test yourself by concealing the Spanish on the right using the cover flap.

¿Tiene la habitación vistas al parque?
<u>tye</u>nay lah abeeta<u>thyon</u>
<u>bees</u>tas al <u>par</u>kay
Does the room have a view over the park?

room	**la habitación** lah abeeta<u>thyon</u>
single room	**la habitación individual** lah abeeta<u>thyon</u> indeebeedwal
double room	**la habitación doble** lah abeeta<u>thyon</u> <u>doblay</u>
bathroom	**el cuarto de baño** el <u>kwar</u>toh day <u>ban</u>yoh
shower	**la ducha** lah <u>doo</u>chah
breakfast	**el desayuno** el desa<u>yoo</u>noh
key	**la llave** lah <u>ya</u>bay
balcony	**el balcón** el bal<u>kon</u>
air-conditioning	**el aire acondicionado** el ah-<u>eer</u>ay akondeethyo<u>na</u>doh

5 Say it

Do you have a single room, please?

For six nights.

Is breakfast included?

Cultural tip Large hotels and paradors are generally the only types of hotels to offer breakfast, but you will generally be charged extra. If your accommodation doesn't provide breakfast, you'll usually find it easy to discover a bar or a café nearby where you can go for "café con leche" in the mornings.

Sí, claro. ¿Cuántas noches?
see, <u>klar</u>oh. <u>kwan</u>tas <u>no</u>ches

Yes, of course. How many nights?

Para tres noches.
<u>par</u>ah tres <u>no</u>ches

For three nights.

Muy bien. Aquí tiene la llave.
mwee byen. ah<u>kee</u> <u>tye</u>nay lah <u>ya</u>bay

Fine. Here's the key.

1 Warm up

Say "Is there...?" and "There isn't...".
(pp.48–9)

What does "¿Le puedo ayudar?" mean?
(pp.54–5)

En el hotel
In the hotel

Although rooms in larger hotels almost always have private bathrooms, there are still some **pensiones** and **hostales** where you will have to share bathroom facilities and in which towels are not supplied. It is always advisable to check what is provided when you make reservations.

2 Match and repeat

Match the numbered items in this hotel bedroom with the Spanish text in the panel and test yourself using the cover flap.

1 **la mesilla de noche**
lah me<u>see</u>yah day <u>no</u>chay

2 **la lámpara**
lah <u>lam</u>parah

3 **el equipo de música**
el e<u>kee</u>poh day <u>moo</u>seekah

4 **las cortinas**
las kor<u>tee</u>nas

5 **el sofá**
el so<u>fah</u>

6 **la almohada**
lah almoh-<u>ah</u>dah

7 **el cojín**
el ko<u>heen</u>

8 **la cama**
lah <u>ka</u>mah

9 **la colcha**
lah <u>kol</u>chah

10 **la manta**
lah <u>man</u>tah

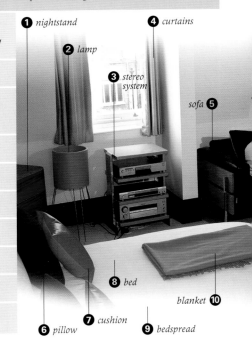

1 nightstand
2 lamp
3 stereo system
4 curtains
5 sofa
6 pillow
7 cushion
8 bed
9 bedspread
10 blanket

Cultural tip When you arrive in your double room, you will usually see one long pillow instead of two individual ones on the bed. This is the usual pillow for a double bed ("cama de matrimonio" or marriage bed). If you don't want to share your bed or pillow, you'll have to ask for "una habitación doble con dos camas" (a double room with two beds) to get a twin room.

3 Useful phrases

Practice these phrases and then test yourself using the cover flap.

The room is too cold/hot.

Hace demasiado frío/calor en la habitación.
<u>ah</u>thay daymas<u>yah</u>doh <u>free</u>oh/<u>ka</u>lor en lah abeeta<u>thyon</u>

There are no towels.

No hay toallas.
noh ah-ee toh-<u>ah</u>yas

I need some soap.

Necesito jabón.
nethe<u>see</u>toh ha<u>bon</u>

The shower doesn't work.

La ducha no funciona.
lah <u>doo</u>chah noh foon<u>thyo</u>nah

The elevator is broken.

El ascensor está roto.
el asthen<u>sor</u> es<u>tah</u> <u>rro</u>toh

4 Put into practice

Practice these phrases and then complete the dialogue in Spanish.

¿Le atienden?
lay at<u>yain</u>den
Can I help you?

Say: I need some pillows.

Necesito almohadas.
nethe<u>see</u>toh almoh-<u>ah</u>das

La camarera se las llevará.
lah kama<u>rai</u>rah say las yeba<u>rah</u>
The maid will bring some.

Say: And the TV doesn't work.

Y la televisión no funciona.
ee lah telebee<u>syon</u> noh foon<u>thyo</u>nah

1 Warm up

How do you ask
"Can I?" (pp.34–5)

Say "The elevator is
broken."(pp.60–1)

Say "I need some
towels". (pp.60–1)

En el cámping
At the campground

Camping is very popular in Spain. The
country's numerous campgrounds are
well organized and operate on a star
system. The local tourist information
office will be able to offer a list of
campgrounds in the area with their
ratings. It is advisable to book in
advance during the summer months.

2 Useful phrases

Learn these phrases and then test yourself
by concealing the Spanish with the cover flap.

¿Puedo alquilar una bicicleta? pwedoh alkeelar oonah beetheekletah	*Can I rent a bicycle?*
¿Es el agua potable? es el ahgwah potablay	*Is this drinking water?*
¿Se permiten hogueras? say permeeten ohgheras	*Are campfires allowed?*
Las radios están prohibidas. las rradyos estan proheebeedas	*Radios are forbidden.*

el doble techo
el doblay taychoh
flysheet

¿Dónde está el grifo?
donday estah el greefoh
Where is the faucet?

la oficina
lah ofeetheenah
office

el contenedor de la basura
el kontenedor day lah basoorah
trash can

3 In conversation

Necesito una plaza para tres noches.
netheseetoh oonah plathah parah tres noches

I need a site for three nights.

Hay una cerca de la piscina.
ah-ee oonah therkah day lah peestheenah

There's one near the swimming pool.

¿Cuánto cuesta para una roulotte?
kwantoh kwestah parah oonah rroolot

How much is it for a camper?

4 Words to remember

Learn these words and then test yourself using the cover flap.

5 Say it

I need a site for four nights.

Can I rent a tent?

Where's the electrical hookup?

campground	**el cámping** el <u>kam</u>peen
tent	**la tienda** lah <u>tyen</u>dah
camper trailer	**la roulotte** lah rroo<u>lot</u>
camper van	**la autocaravana** la ah-ootokara<u>ba</u>nah
site	**la plaza** lah <u>plath</u>ah
campfire	**la hoguera** lah oh<u>gh</u>erah
drinking water	**el agua potable** el <u>ah</u>gwah po<u>tab</u>lay
garbage	**la basura** lah ba<u>soo</u>rah
stove fuel	**el camping-gas** el <u>kam</u>peen gas
showers	**las duchas** las <u>doo</u>chas
sleeping bag	**el saco de dormir** el <u>sa</u>koh day dor<u>meer</u>
air mattress	**la colchoneta** lah kolcho<u>ne</u>tah
groundsheet	**el suelo aislante** el <u>swe</u>loh ah-ees<u>lan</u>tay

los aseos
los a<u>say</u>os
restrooms

el punto de luz
el <u>poon</u>toh day looth
electrical hookup

la cuerda
lah <u>kwer</u>dah
guy rope

la clavija
la kla<u>bee</u>hah
tent peg

Cincuenta euros. Una noche por adelantado.
thee<u>nkwen</u>tah eh-<u>oo</u>ros.
<u>oo</u>nah <u>no</u>chay por adelan<u>ta</u>doh

Fifty euros. One night in advance.

¿Puedo alquilar una barbacoa?
<u>pwe</u>doh alkee<u>lar oo</u>nah barba<u>koh</u>-ah

Can I rent a barbecue grill?

Sí, pero tiene que dejar una señal.
see, <u>pe</u>roh <u>tye</u>nay kay de<u>har oo</u>nah se<u>nyal</u>

Yes, but you must pay a deposit.

1 Warm up

How do you say "hot" and "cold"? (pp.60–1)

What is the Spanish for "room," "bed," and "pillow"? (pp.60–1)

Descripciones
Descriptions

Adjectives are words used to describe things. In Spanish you generally put the adjective after the thing it describes in the same gender and number: **una bebida fría** (*a cold drink*, feminine singular); **un café frío** (*a cold coffee*, masculine singular); **dos bebidas frías** (*two cold drinks*, feminine plural).

2 Words to remember

Adjectives change depending on whether the thing described is masculine (**el**) or feminine (**la**). Generally, a final "o" changes to "a" in the feminine, but if the adjective ends with "e" (such as **grande**) it doesn't change for the feminine. For the plural, just add an "s."

duro/dura dooroh/doorah	*hard*
blando/blanda blandoh/blandah	*soft*
caliente kalyaintay	*hot*
frío/fría freeoh/freeah	*cold*
grande granday	*big*
pequeño/pequeña pekenyoh/pekenyah	*small*
bonito/bonita boneetoh/boneetah	*beautiful*
feo/fea feh-oh/feh-ah	*ugly*
ruidoso/ruidosa rrweedosoh/ rrweedosah	*noisy*
tranquilo/tranquila trankeeloh/trankeelah	*quiet*
bueno/buena bwenoh/bwenah	*good*
malo/mala maloh/malah	*bad*
lento/lenta lentoh/lentah	*slow*
rápido/rápida rrapeedoh/rrapeedah	*fast*

las montañas altas
las montanyas altas
high mountains

la tienda pequeña
lah tyaindah pekenyah
small shop

el coche viejo
el koche bee-ayhoh
old car

la calle tranquila
lah kayay trankeelah
quiet road

El pueblo es muy bonito.
el pwebloh es mwee boneetoh
The village is very beautiful.

3 Useful phrases

Learn these phrases. Note that you can emphasize a description by using **muy** (*very*), **demasiado** (*too*), or **más** (*more*) before the adjective.

This coffee is cold.

Este café está frío.
estay kafay estah
free-oh

My room is very noisy.

Mi habitación es muy ruidosa.
mee abeetathyon es mwee rrweedosah

My car is too small.

Mi coche es demasiado pequeño.
mee koche es demasyahdoh pekenyoh

I need a softer bed.

Necesito una cama más blanda.
netheseetoh oonah kamah mas blandah

4 Put into practice

Join in this conversation. Cover up the text on the right and complete the dialogue in Spanish. Check and repeat if necessary.

Ésta es la habitación.
estah es lah abeetathyon
This is the bedroom.

Say: The view is very beautiful.

La vista es muy bonita.
lah beestah es mwee boneetah

El cuarto de baño está por ahí.
el kwartoh day banyoh estah por ah-ee
The bathroom is over there.

Say: It is too small.

Es demasiado pequeño.
es demasyahdoh pekenyoh

No tenemos otra.
noh tenaymos otrah
We don't have another one.

Say: It doesn't matter. We'll take the room.

No importa. Nos quedamos con la habitación.
noh importah. nos kedamos kon lah abeetathyon

Respuestas
Answers
Cover with flap

Repase y repita
Review and repeat

1 Descriptions

1 **caliente**
kal<u>yain</u>tay

2 **pequeña**
pe<u>ken</u>yah

3 **frío**
<u>free</u>-oh

4 **grande**
<u>gran</u>day

5 **tranquila**
tran<u>kee</u>lah

1 Descriptions

Put the word in brackets into Spanish. Use the correct masculine or feminine form.

1 El agua está demasiado ____ (hot).

2 La cama es muy ____ (small).

3 El café está ____ (cold).

4 Este cuarto de baño es más ____ (big).

5 Quisiera una habitación más ____ (quiet).

2 Campground

1 **el punto de luz**
el <u>poon</u>toh day looth

2 **la tienda**
lah <u>tyain</u>dah

3 **el contenedor de la basura**
el konte<u>ned</u>or day lah ba<u>soo</u>rah

4 **la cuerda**
lah <u>kwer</u>dah

5 **los aseos**
los a<u>say</u>os

6 **la roulotte**
lah rroo<u>lot</u>

2 Campground

Name these items you might find in a campground.

1 *electrical hookup* **3** *trash can*

2 *tent*

guy rope **4**

3 At the hotel

You are booking a room in a hotel. Follow the conversation, replying in Spanish where you can see the English prompts.

¿Qué desean?
1 *Do you have any vacancies?*

Sí, una habitación doble.
2 *Do you accept pets?*

Sí. ¿Cuántas noches?
3 *Three nights.*

Son ciento cuarenta euros.
4 *Is breakfast included?*

Sí. Aquí tiene la llave.
5 *Thank you very much.*

3 At the hotel

1 **¿Tiene habitaciones libres?**
tyenay abeeta-thyones leebres

2 **¿Aceptan animales de compañía?**
atheptan aneemales day kompanyeeah

3 **Tres noches.**
tres noches

4 **¿El desayuno está incluido?**
el desayoonoh estah inklooeedoh

5 **Muchas gracias.**
moochas grathyas

4 Negatives

Make these sentences negative using the verb in brackets.

1 Yo ____ hijos. (tener)

2 Ellos ____ a Madrid mañana. (ir)

3 Él ____ un café. (querer)

4 Yo ____ el metro. (coger)

5 La vista ____ muy bonita. (ser)

4 Negatives

1 **no tengo**
noh tengoh

2 **no van**
noh ban

3 **no quiere**
noh kyairay

4 **no cojo**
noh kohoh

5 **no es**
no es

5 *restrooms*

6 *camper*

1 Warm up

Ask "How do I get to the station?" (pp.50–1)

Say "Turn left at the traffic lights" and "The station is across from the café." (pp.50–1)

De compras
Shopping

Small, traditional shops are still very common in Spain. But you can also find big supermarkets and shopping centers on the outskirts of cities. Local markets selling fresh, local produce can be found everywhere. Ask which day is market day at the **oficina de información turística** (*tourist office*).

2 Match and repeat

Match the stores numbered 1 to 9 below and right to the Spanish in the panel. Then test yourself using the cover flap.

1 **la panadería**
lah panadaireeah

2 **la pastelería**
lah pastaylaireeah

3 **el estanco**
el estankoh

4 **la carnicería**
lah karnee-thaireeah

5 **la charcutería**
lah charkoo-taireeah

6 **la librería**
lah leebraireeah

7 **la pescadería**
lah peskadaireeah

8 **la joyería**
lah hoyereeah

9 **el banco**
el bankoh

❶ *bread shop*

❷ *bakery*

❹ *butcher*

❺ *delicatessen*

❼ *fishmonger*

❽ *jeweler*

Cultural tip If you want an everyday bar of soap or a tube of toothpaste, you need to go to a "droguería" (drugstore) rather than the "farmacia" (pharmacy). The "estanco" (tobacconist) is the place for all sorts of tobacco products and stamps. "Papelerías" cater for all your stationery needs. Most Spanish shops offer a free gift-wrapping service; you only need to ask: "¿Me lo envuelve para regalo?" (May I have it gift-wrapped?).

3 Words to remember

Familiarize yourself with these words and test yourself using the flap.

¿Dónde está la floristería?
<u>don</u>day es<u>tah</u> lah floreestai<u>ree</u>ah
Where is the florist?

❸ *tobacconist*

❻ *bookstore*

❾ *bank*

hardware store	**la ferretería**	lah ferretai<u>ree</u>ah
antique shop	**el anticuario**	el antee<u>kwa</u>reeoh
hairdresser	**la peluquería**	lah pelookai<u>ree</u>ah
greengrocer	**la verdulería**	lah berdoolai<u>ree</u>ah
post office	**la oficina de correos**	lah ofee<u>thee</u>nah day ko<u>rra</u>yos
shoe store	**la zapatería**	lah thapatai<u>ree</u>ah
dry-cleaner	**la tintorería**	lah teentorai<u>ree</u>ah
grocery	**el ultramarinos**	el ooltrama<u>ree</u>nos

4 Useful phrases

Familiarize yourself with these phrases.

Where is the hairdresser?	**¿Dónde está la peluquería?** <u>don</u>day es<u>tah</u> lah pelookai<u>ree</u>ah
Where do I pay?	**¿Dónde se paga?** <u>don</u>day say <u>pa</u>gah
I'm just looking, thank you.	**Sólo estoy mirando, gracias.** <u>so</u>loh es<u>toy</u> mee<u>ran</u>doh <u>gra</u>thyas
Do you sell phone cards?	**¿Tiene tarjetas telefónicas?** <u>tye</u>nay tar<u>he</u>tas telefo<u>nee</u>kas
May I have two of those?	**¿Me pone dos de éstos?** may <u>po</u>nay dos day <u>es</u>tos
Can I place an order?	**¿Puedo hacer un pedido?** <u>pwe</u>doh ah<u>ther</u> oon pe<u>dee</u>doh

5 Say it

Where is the bank?

Do you sell cheese?

Where do I pay?

En el mercado
At the market

1 Warm up

What is Spanish for 40, 56, 77, 82, and 94? (pp.10–11 and pp.30–1)

Say "I'd like a big room." (pp.64–5)

Ask "Do you have a small car?" (pp.64–5)

Spain uses the metric system of weights and measures, so you will need to ask for produce in kilograms or grams. Some larger items, such as melons or pineapples, tend to be sold by **la pieza** (as single items); other items, such as lettuce, may be sold in twos or threes.

2 Match and repeat

Match the numbered items in this scene with the text in the panel.

1 **los tomates**
   los to<u>ma</u>tes

2 **las judías**
   las hoo<u>dee</u>as

3 **los champiñones**
   los champee<u>nyo</u>nes

4 **las uvas**
   las <u>oo</u>bas

5 **los pepinos**
   los pe<u>pee</u>nos

6 **las alcachofas**
   las alka<u>cho</u>fas

7 **los guisantes**
   los ghee<u>san</u>tes

8 **los pimientos**
   los peem<u>yain</u>tos

1 tomatoes

5 cucumbers   peas 7

artichokes 6   peppers 8

3 In conversation

Quisiera tomates.
kee<u>syair</u>ah to<u>ma</u>tes

I'd like some tomatoes.

¿De los grandes o de los pequeños?
day los <u>gran</u>des oh day los pe<u>ken</u>yos

The large ones or the small ones?

Dos kilos de los pequeños, por favor.
dos <u>kee</u>los day los pe<u>ken</u>yos, por fa<u>bor</u>

Two kilos of the small ones, please.

SHOPPING **71**

Cultural tip Spain uses the common European currency, the euro, which is divided into 100 "centimos." Spanish-speaking countries in Central and South America all have their own currencies. Argentina, Chile, Uruguay, Colombia, and Mexico all call their currency the peso, which is divided into 100 "centavos."

 ❷ *beans*

❸ *mushrooms*

❹ *grapes*

4 Useful phrases

Learn these phrases. Then cover up the answers on the right. Read the English under the pictures and say the phrase in Spanish as shown on the right.

That sausage is too expensive.

Esa salchicha es demasiado cara.
ehsah salcheechah es demasyahdoh karah

How much is that one?

¿A cuánto está esa?
ah kwantoh estah ehsa

5 Say it

Two kilos of peas, please.

The mushrooms are too expensive.

How much are the grapes?

That's all.

Eso es todo.
ehsoh es todoh

¿Algo más, señorita?
algoh mas, senyoreetah

Anything else, miss?

Eso es todo, gracias. ¿Cuánto es?
ehsoh es todoh, grathyas. kwantoh es

That's all, thank you. How much?

Tres cincuenta.
tres theenkwentah

Three-fifty.

1 Warm up

What are these items you could buy in a supermarket?
(pp.24–5)

la carne
el pescado
el queso
el zumo
el vino
el agua

En el supermercado
At the supermarket

Prices in supermarkets are usually lower than in smaller shops. They offer all kinds of products, with larger out-of-town **hipermercados** carrying clothes, household goods, lawn furniture, and home improvement products.

2 Match and repeat

Look at the numbered product categories and match them to the Spanish words in the panel on the left.

1 **los productos del hogar**
los pro*dook*tos del oh*gar*

2 **la fruta**
lah *froo*tah

3 **las bebidas**
las be*bee*das

4 **los platos preparados**
los *pla*tos prepa*ra*dos

5 **los productos de belleza**
los pro*dook*tos day be*yeth*ah

6 **los productos lácteos**
los pro*dook*tos *lak*teh-os

7 **la verdura**
lah ber*door*ah

8 **los congelados**
los konhe*la*dos

household products ❶

fruit ❷

drinks ❸

prepared meals ❹

vegetables ❼

frozen foods ❽

Cultural tip It is not usually possible to take unweighed fruit and vegetables sold by the kilo directly to the supermarket checkout. There is usually a separate counter or a self-service weighing machine.

3 Useful phrases

Learn these phrases and then test yourself using the cover flap.

May I have a bag, please?	**¿Me da una bolsa, por favor?** may dah <u>oo</u>nah <u>bol</u>sah, por fa<u>bor</u>

Where are the drinks?	**¿Dónde están las bebidas?** <u>don</u>day es<u>tan</u> las be<u>bee</u>das

Where is the check-out, please?	**¿Dónde está la caja, por favor?** <u>don</u>day es<u>tah</u> lah <u>ka</u>hah, por fa<u>bor</u>

Please type in your PIN.	**Por favor, meta su PIN.** por fa<u>bor</u>, <u>me</u>tah soo peen

4 Words to remember

Learn these words and then test yourself using the cover flap.

5 *beauty products*

6 *dairy products*

bread	**el pan** el pan
milk	**la leche** lah <u>le</u>chay
butter	**la mantequilla** lah mante<u>kee</u>yah
ham	**el jamón** el ha<u>mon</u>
salt	**la sal** lah sal
pepper	**la pimienta** lah pee<u>myain</u>tah
laundry detergent	**el jabón de lavadora** el ha<u>bon</u> day laba<u>dor</u>ah
toilet paper	**el papel higiénico** el pa<u>pel</u> eeh<u>yain</u>eekoh
diapers	**los pañales** los pan<u>ya</u>les

5 Say it

Where are the dairy products?

May I have some cheese, please?

Where are the frozen foods?

La ropa y los zapatos
Clothes and shoes

1 Warm up

Say "I'd like...".
(pp.22–3)

Ask "Do you have...?"
(pp.14–15)

Say "38," "42," and
"46." (pp.10–11 and
pp.30–1)

Say "big," "small,"
"bigger," and
"smaller." (pp.64–5)

Clothes and shoes are measured in metric sizes from 36 upward. Even allowing for conversion of sizes, Spanish clothes tend to be cut smaller than American ones. Clothes size is **la talla** but shoe size is **el número**.

2 Match and repeat

Match the numbered items of clothing to the Spanish words in the panel on the left. Test yourself using the cover flap.

1 **la camisa**
  lah kameesah

2 **la corbata**
  lah korbatah

3 **la chaqueta**
  lah chaketah

4 **el bolsillo**
  el bolseeyoh

5 **la manga**
  lah mangah

6 **el pantalón**
  el pantalon

7 **la falda**
  lah faldah

8 **las medias**
  las medyas

9 **los zapatos**
  los thapatos

shirt ❶

tie ❷

jacket ❸

pocket ❹

sleeve ❺

pants ❻

Cultural tip As in most of mainland Europe, Spain uses the continental system of sizes. Women's clothes sizes usually range from 36 (US 6) through to 46 (US 18), and shoe sizes from 37 (US 5½) to 45 (US 12). For men's shirts, a size 41 is a 16-inch collar, 43 is a 17-inch collar, and 45 is an 18-inch collar.

3 Useful phrases

Practice these phrases and then test yourself using the cover flap.

Do you have a larger size?	**¿Tiene una talla más grande?** tyenay oonah tayah mas granday

It's not what I want.	**No es lo que quiero.** noh es loh kay kyairoh
I'll take the pink one.	**Me quedo con el rosa.** may kedoh kon el rrosah

4 Words to remember

Colors are adjectives (pp.64–5) and in most cases have a masculine and a feminine form. The feminine is usually formed by substituting an "a" for the final "o."

red	**rojo/roja** rrohoh/rrohah
white	**blanco/blanca** blankoh/blankah
blue	**azul** athool
yellow	**amarillo/amarilla** amareeyoh/amareeyah
green	**verde** berday
black	**negro/negra** negroh/negrah

7 *skirt*

8 *pantyhose*

9 *shoes*

5 Say it

What shoe size?

Do you have a black jacket?

Do you have a size 38?

Do you have a smaller size?

Repase y repita
Review and repeat

1 Market

1 **las alcachofas**
las alka<u>cho</u>fas

2 **los tomates**
los to<u>ma</u>tes

3 **los guisantes**
los ghee<u>san</u>tes

4 **los pimientos**
los pee<u>myain</u>tos

5 **las judías**
las hoo<u>dee</u>eah

1 Market

Name the numbered vegetables in Spanish.

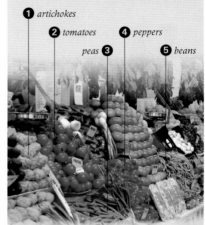

❶ *artichokes*
❷ *tomatoes* ❹ *peppers*
peas ❸ ❺ *beans*

2 Description

1 *The shoes are too expensive.*

2 *My room is very small.*

3 *I need a softer bed.*

2 Description

What do these sentences mean?

1 **Los zapatos son demasiados caros.**

2 **Mi habitación es muy pequeña.**

3 **Necesito una cama más blanda.**

3 Stores

1 **la panadería**
lah panadai<u>ree</u>ah

2 **la joyería**
lah hoyeh<u>ree</u>ah

3 **la librería**
lah leebrai<u>ree</u>ah

4 **la pescadería**
lah peskadai<u>ree</u>ah

5 **la pastelería**
lah pastaylai<u>ree</u>ah

6 **la carnicería**
lah karneethai<u>ree</u>ah

3 Stores

Name the numbered shops in Spanish.
Then check your answers.

❶ *bread shop* ❷ *jeweler* ❸ *bookstore*

❹ *fishmonger* ❺ *bakery* ❻ *butcher*

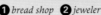

Respuestas
Answers
Cover with flap

4 Supermarket

What is the Spanish for the numbered product categories?

1 household products

2 beauty products

3 drinks

4 dairy products

5 vegetables

4 Supermarket

1 **los productos del hogar**
los pro*dook*tos del oh*gar*

2 **los productos de belleza**
los pro*dook*tos day be*yet*hah

3 **las bebidas**
las be*bee*das

4 **los productos lácteos**
los pro*dook*tos *lak*teh-os

5 **la verdura**
lah ber*door*ah

5 Museum

Follow this conversation, replying in Spanish following the English prompts.

Buenos días. ¿Qué desean?
1 *I'd like five tickets.*

Son setenta y cinco euros.
2 *That's very expensive!*

No hacemos descuentos a los niños.
3 *How much is a guide?*

Quince euros.
4 *Good. And five tickets, please.*

Noventa euros, por favor.
5 *Here you are. Where are the restrooms?*

A la derecha.
6 *Thank you very much.*

5 Museum

1 **Quisiera cinco entradas.**
kee*syair*ah *theen*koh en*tra*das

2 **¡Es muy caro!**
es mwee *kar*oh

3 **¿Cuánto cuesta una guía?**
*kwan*toh *kwes*tah *oo*nah *ghee*ah

4 **Bien. Y cinco entradas, por favor.**
Byen. ee *theen*koh en*tra*das, por fa*bor*

5 **Aquí tiene. ¿Dónde están los servicios?**
ah*kee* *tye*nay. *don*day es*tan* los ser*bee*thyos

6 **Muchas gracias.**
*moo*chas *grath*yas

Las ocupaciones
Jobs

1 Warm up

Say "from which platform?" (pp.38–9)

What is the Spanish for the following family members: sister, brother, mother, father, son, and daughter? (pp.10–11)

Some occupations have commonly used feminine alternatives—for example, **enfermero** (*male nurse*) and **enfermera** (*female nurse*). Others remain the same. When you describe your occupation, you don't use **un/una** (*a*), saying simply **soy abogado** (*I'm a lawyer*), for example.

2 Words to remember: jobs

Familiarize yourself with these words and test yourself using the flap. The feminine alternative is shown in brackets.

médico medeekoh	*doctor*
dentista denteestah	*dentist*
enfermero/-a enfermairoh/-ah	*nurse*
profesor/-sora profaysor/-sorah	*teacher*
abogado/-a abogadoh/-ah	*lawyer*
contable kontablay	*accountant*
diseñador/-dora deesenyador/-dorah	*designer*
consultor/-a konsooltor/-ah	*consultant*
secretario/-a sekraytareeoh(-ah)	*secretary*
comerciante komerthyantay	*shopkeeper*
electricista elektreetheestah	*electrician*
fontanero/-a fontanairoh/-ah	*plumber*
cocinero/-a kotheenairoh/-ah	*cook/chef*
albañil albanyeel	*handyman*
autónomo/-a aootohnomoh/-ah	*self-employed*

Soy fontanero.
soy fontanairoh
I'm a plumber.

Es estudiante.
es estoodyantay
She is a student.

3 Put into practice

Join in this conversation. Read the Spanish on the left and follow the instructions to make your reply. Then test yourself.

¿Cuál es su profesión?
kwal es soo profesyon
What do you do?

Say: I am a consultant.

Soy consultor.
soy konsooltor

¿Para qué empresa trabaja?
parah kay empresah trabahah
What company do you work for?

Say: I'm self-employed.

Soy autónomo.
soy aootohnomoh

¡Qué interesante!
kay intairaysantay
How interesting!

Say: And what is your profession?

¿Y cuál es su profesión?
ee kwal es soo profesyon

Soy dentista.
soy denteestah
I'm a dentist.

Say: My sister is a dentist, too.

Mi hermana es dentista también.
mee airrmanah es denteestah tambyen

---

4 Words to remember: workplace

Familiarize yourself with these words and test yourself.

La oficina central está en Madrid.
lah ofeetheenah thentral estah en madreed
Headquarters is in Madrid.

branch	**la sucursal** lah sookoorsal
department	**el departamento** el departamaintoh
manager	**el jefe** el hefay
employee	**el empleado** el emplay-ahdoh
reception	**la recepción** lah rrethepthyon
trainee	**el aprendiz** el ahprendeeth

La oficina
The office

An office environment or business situation has its own vocabulary in any language, but there are many items that are virtually universal. Be aware that Spanish computer keyboards have a different layout from the standard "QWERTY" convention; they also include **ñ**, vowels with accents, **¡**, and **¿**.

2 Words to remember

Familiarize yourself with these words. Read them aloud several times and try to memorize them. Conceal the Spanish with the cover flap and test yourself.

el monitor el mone<u>e</u>tor	*monitor*
el ratón el rra<u>ton</u>	*mouse*
el correo electrónico el ko<u>rra</u>yoh elek<u>tro</u>neekoh	*email*
el internet el eenter<u>net</u>	*Internet*
la contraseña lah kontra<u>se</u>nyah	*password*
la mensajería de voz lah mensahe<u>ree</u>ah day both	*voicemail*
el fax el fax	*fax machine*
la fotocopiadora lah fotokopy<u>a</u>dorah	*photocopier*
la agenda lah ah-<u>hen</u>dah	*planner*
la tarjeta de visita lah tar<u>he</u>tah day bee<u>see</u>tah	*business card*
la reunión lah reh-oony<u>on</u>	*meeting*
la conferencia lah konfair<u>en</u>theeah	*conference*
el orden del día el <u>or</u>den del <u>dee</u>ah	*agenda*

1 *lamp*

screen **4**

2 *stapler*

telephone **3**

pen **10**

notepad **11**

drawer **12**

3 Useful phrases

Learn these phrases and then test yourself using the cover flap.

	I need to make some photocopies.	**Necesito hacer unas fotocopias.** netheseetoh ahther oonas fotokopyas
	I'd like to arrange an appointment.	**Quisiera organizar una cita.** keesyairah organeethar oonah theetah
	I want to send an email.	**Quiero mandar un correo electrónico.** kyairoh mandar oon korrayoh elektroneekoh

4 Match and repeat

Match the numbered items to the Spanish words on the left.

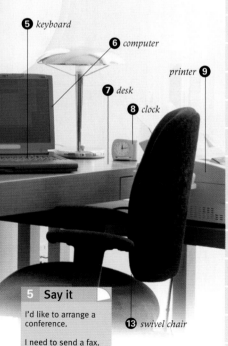

5 *keyboard*

6 *computer*

printer 9

7 *desk*

8 *clock*

13 *swivel chair*

1 **la lámpara**
lah lamparah

2 **la grapadora**
lah grapadohrah

3 **el teléfono**
el telefonoh

4 **la pantalla**
lah pantayah

5 **el teclado**
el tekladoh

6 **el ordenador**
el ordenador

7 **la mesa de escritorio**
lah mesah day eskreetoryoh

8 **el reloj**
el rrelokh

9 **la impresora**
lah impresorah

10 **el bolígrafo**
el boleegrafoh

11 **el bloc**
el blok

12 **el cajón**
el kahon

13 **la silla giratoria**
lah seeyah heeratoreeah

5 Say it

I'd like to arrange a conference.

I need to send a fax.

Do you have email?

1 Warm up

Say "library" and "How interesting!" (pp.48–9, pp.78–9)

Ask "What is your profession?" and answer "I'm an engineer." (pp.78–9)

El mundo académico
Academic world

In Spain students are selected for a bachelor's degree (**una licenciatura**) by an average of secondary school grades and an exam. After graduation some students go on to **un máster** (master's degree) or **un doctorado** (PhD).

2 Useful phrases

Practice these phrases and then test yourself using the cover flap.

¿Cuál es su especialidad? kwal es soo espetheeahleedad	*What is your field?*	
Hago investigación en bioquímica. ahgoh inbesteegathyon en beeohkeemeekah	*I am doing research in biochemistry.*	
Soy licenciado en derecho. soy leethentheeahdoh en derechoh	*I have a degree in law.*	
Voy a dar una conferencia sobre arquitectura. boy ah dar oonah konfairayntheeah sobreh arkeetektoorah	*I'm going to give a lecture on architecture.*	

3 In conversation

Hola, soy la profesora Fernández.
o-lah, soy lah profaysorah fernandeth

Hello, I'm Professor Fernandez.

¿De qué universidad es usted?
deh keh ooneeberseedad es oosted

What university are you from?

De la Universidad de Murcia.
deh lah ooneeberseedad deh moortheeah

From the University of Murcia.

4 Words to remember

Familiarize yourself with these words and then test yourself.

conference/lecture	**la conferencia** lah konfair<u>ain</u>theeah
trade fair	**la feria** lah f<u>e</u>reeah
seminar	**el seminario** el semee<u>na</u>ryoh
lecture hall	**el anfiteatro** el anfeetay-<u>ah</u>troh
conference room	**la sala de conferencias** lah <u>sah</u>lah deh konfer<u>ain</u>theeas
exhibition	**la exposición** lah eksposeethy<u>on</u>
library	**la biblioteca** lah bibleeo<u>te</u>kah
assistant professor	**el profesor de universidad** el profa<u>yor</u> deh ooneeberse<u>e</u>dad
professor	**el catedrático** el kate<u>dra</u>teekoh
medicine	**medicina** medeet<u>hee</u>nah
science	**ciencias** <u>thyain</u>theeas
literature	**literatura** leetaira<u>too</u>rah
engineering	**ingeniería** inhainyair<u>ee</u>ah

Tenemos un stand en la feria.
ten<u>e</u>mos oon es<u>tand</u> en la f<u>e</u>reeah
We have a stand at the trade fair.

5 Say it

I'm doing research in medicine.

I have a degree in literature.

She's the professor.

¿Cuál es su especialidad?
kwal es soo espethyalee<u>dad</u>

What's your field?

Hago investigación en ingeniería.
<u>ah</u>goh inbesteegathy<u>on</u> en inhenyair<u>ee</u>ah

I'm doing research in engineering.

¡Qué interesante! Yo también.
keh intairay<u>san</u>tay, yoh tambee<u>ayn</u>

How interesting! I am, too.

Ask "Can I ...?"
(pp.34–5)

Say "I want to send an email." (pp.80–1)

Say "I'd like to arrange an appointment." (pp.80–1)

Los negocios
In business

You will receive a more friendly reception and make a good impression if you make the effort to begin a meeting with a short introduction in Spanish, even if your vocabulary is limited. After that, all parties will probably be happy to continue the proceedings in English.

2 Words to remember

Familiarize yourself with these words and then test yourself by covering the Spanish with the flap.

el cliente
el klyaintay
client

el programa el programah	*schedule*
la entrega lah entraygah	*delivery*
el pago el pahgoh	*payment*
el presupuesto el praysoopwestoh	*budget/estimate*
el precio el praythyoh	*price*
el documento el dokoomentoh	*document*
la factura lah faktoorah	*invoice*
la propuesta lah propwestah	*proposal*
los beneficios los baynayfeethyos	*profits*
las ventas las bentas	*sales*
los números los noomeros	*figures*

el informe
el informay
report

Cultural tip A long lunch with wine is still a regular feature of doing business in Spain. As a visiting client you can expect to be taken out to a restaurant, and as a supplier you should consider entertaining your business customers.

3 Useful phrases

Practice these useful business phrases and then test yourself using the cover flap.

¿Firmamos el contrato?
feer<u>ma</u>mos el kon<u>tra</u>toh
Shall we sign the contract?

el ejecutivo
el eh-hekoo<u>tee</u>boh
executive

Please send me the contract.

Me manda el contrato, por favor.
may <u>man</u>dah el kon<u>tra</u>toh, por fa<u>bor</u>

Have we agreed on a schedule?

¿Hemos acordado un programa?
<u>eh</u>mos akor<u>da</u>doh oon pro<u>gra</u>mah

When can you make the delivery?

¿Cuándo puede hacer la entrega?
<u>kwan</u>doh <u>pwe</u>day a<u>ther</u> lah en<u>tre</u>gah

What's the budget?

¿Cuál es el presupuesto?
<u>kwal</u> es el praysoo<u>pwes</u>toh

Can you send me the invoice?

¿Me puede mandar la factura?
may <u>pwe</u>day man<u>dar</u> lah fak<u>too</u>rah

el contrato
el kon<u>tra</u>toh
contract

4 Say it

Can you send me the estimate?

Have we agreed on a price?

What are the profits?

Repase y repita
Review and repeat

1 At the office

1 **la grapadora**
lah grapa<u>do</u>rah

2 **la lámpara**
lah <u>lam</u>parah

3 **el ordenador**
el ordena<u>dor</u>

4 **el bolígrafo**
el bo<u>lee</u>grafoh

5 **el reloj**
el rre<u>lokh</u>

6 **el bloc**
el blok

7 **la mesa de escritorio**
lah <u>me</u>sah day eskree<u>to</u>ryoh

1 At the office

Name these items.

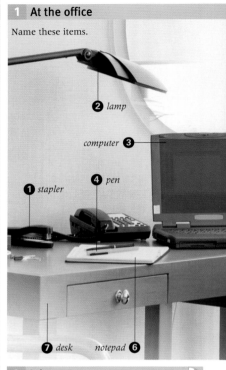

2 *lamp*

computer 3

1 *stapler*   4 *pen*

7 *desk*   *notepad* 6

2 Jobs

1 **médico**
<u>me</u>deekoh

2 **fontanero(-a)**
fonta<u>nair</u>oh(-ah)

3 **comerciante**
komer<u>thyan</u>tay

4 **contable**
kon<u>ta</u>blay

5 **estudiante**
estoo<u>dyan</u>tay

6 **abogado(-a)**
abo<u>ga</u>doh(-ah)

2 Jobs

What are these jobs in Spanish?

1 *doctor*

2 *plumber*

3 *shopkeeper*

4 *accountant*

5 *student*

6 *lawyer*

clock **5**

3 Work

Answer these questions following the English prompts.

¿Para qué empresa trabaja?
1 *Say: I am self-employed.*

¿En qué universidad está?
2 *Say: I'm at the University of Salamanca.*

¿Cuál es su especialidad?
3 *Say: I'm doing research in medicine.*

¿Hemos acordado un programa?
4 *Say: Yes, my secretary has the schedule.*

3 Work

1 **Soy autónomo.**
soy ao<u>to</u>nomoh

2 **Estoy en la Universidad de Salamanca.**
es<u>toy</u> en lah ooneeberseedad day sala<u>man</u>kah

3 **Hago investigación en medicina.**
<u>ah</u>goh inbesteegathy<u>on</u> en medee<u>thee</u>nah

4 **Sí. mi secretaria tiene el programa.**
see. mee sekre<u>ta</u>reeah <u>tye</u>nay el pro<u>gra</u>mah

4 How much?

Answer the question with the amount shown in brackets.

1 **¿Cuánto cuesta el desayuno?** (€3.50)

2 **¿Cuánto cuesta la habitación?** (€47)

3 **¿Cuánto cuesta un kilo de tomates?** (€3.25)

4 **¿Cuánto cuesta un plaza para cuatro noches?** (€60)

4 How much?

1 **Son tres euros cincuenta.**
son tres eh-<u>oo</u>ros theen<u>kwen</u>tah

2 **Son cuarenta y siete euros.**
son kwa<u>ren</u>tah ee <u>seeay</u>tay eh-<u>oo</u>ros

3 **Son tres euros veinticinco.**
son tres eh-<u>oo</u>ros beyntee<u>theen</u>koh

4 **Son sesenta euros.**
son se<u>sen</u>tah eh-<u>oo</u>ros

Say "I'm allergic to nuts." (pp.24–5)

Say the verb "tener" (to have) in all its forms: yo, tú, él/ella, nosotros(-as), vosotros(-as), ellos (-as). (pp.14–15)

En la farmacia
At the pharmacy

Spanish pharmacists are qualified to give advice and sell over-the-counter medicines, as well as dispensing prescription medicines. There is generally a **farmacia de guardia** (duty pharmacy) to provide 24-hour service in every town—a list is displayed in every pharmacy.

2 Match and repeat

Match the numbered items to the Spanish words in the panel on the left and test yourself using the cover flap.

1 **la venda**
lah <u>ben</u>dah

2 **el jarabe**
el ha<u>ra</u>bay

3 **las gotas**
las <u>go</u>tas

4 **la tirita**
lah tee<u>ree</u>tah

5 **la jeringuilla**
lah hereen<u>ghee</u>yah

6 **la crema**
lah <u>kre</u>mah

7 **el supositorio**
el soopos<u>eeto</u>ryoh

8 **la pastilla**
lah pas<u>tee</u>yah

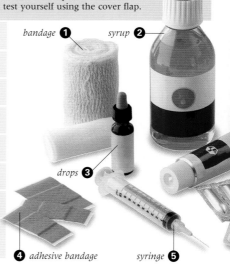

bandage ❶   *syrup* ❷

drops ❸

❹ *adhesive bandage*   *syringe* ❺

3 In conversation

Buenos días, señor. ¿Qué desea?
<u>bwe</u>nos <u>dee</u>yas, sen<u>yor</u>. kay de<u>say</u>ah

Good morning, sir. What would you like?

Tengo dolor de estómago.
<u>ten</u>goh do<u>lor</u> day es<u>to</u>magoh

I have a stomachache.

¿Tiene diarrea?
<u>tye</u>nay deeah<u>rra</u>yah

Do you have diarrhea?

4 Words to remember

Familiarize yourself with these words and test yourself using the flap.

Tengo dolor de cabeza.
tengoh dolor day kabethah
I have a headache.

headache	**el dolor de cabeza** el dolor day kabethah
stomachache	**el dolor de estómago** el dolor day estomagoh
diarrhea	**la diarrea** lah deeahrrayah
cold	**el resfriado** el rresfreeahdoh
cough	**la tos** lah tos
sunburn	**la insolación** lah eensolatheeyon
toothache	**el dolor de muelas** el dolor day mwelas

6 Say it

I have a cold.

Do you have that as a cream?

He has a toothache.

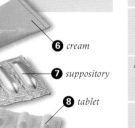

6 *cream*

7 *suppository*

8 *tablet*

5 Useful phrases

Practice these phrases and then test yourself using the cover flap.

I have a sunburn.	**Tengo una insolación.** tengoh oonah eensolatheeyon
Do you have that as a syrup?	**¿Lo tiene en jarabe?** loh tyenay en harabay
I'm allergic to penicillin.	**Soy alérgico a la penicilina.** soy alerheekoh ah lah peneetheeleenah

No, pero tengo dolor de cabeza.
noh, peroh tengoh dolor day kabethah

No, but I have a headache.

Aquí tiene.
ahkee tyenay

Here you are.

¿Lo tiene en pastilla?
loh tyenay en pasteeyah

Do you have this as pills?

1 Warm up

Say " I have a toothache" and "I have a sunburn." (pp.88–9)

Say the Spanish for "red," "green," "black," and "yellow." (pp.74–5)

El cuerpo
The body

You are most likely to need to refer to parts of the body in the context of illness—for example, when describing aches and pains to a doctor. The most common phrases for talking about discomfort are **Tengo un dolor en la/el...** (*I have a pain in the...*) and **Me duele la/el...** (*My ... hurts me*).

2 Match and repeat: body

Match the numbered parts of the body with the list on the left. Test yourself by using the cover flap.

1 **la mano**
lah manoh

2 **la cabeza**
lah kabethah

3 **el hombro**
el ombroh

4 **el codo**
el kodoh

5 **el pelo**
el peloh

6 **el brazo**
el brathoh

7 **el cuello**
el kweyoh

8 **el pecho**
el pechoh

9 **el estómago**
el estomagoh

10 **la pierna**
lah pyairnah

11 **la rodilla**
lah rrodeeyah

12 **el pie**
el pee-ay

hand ❶

head ❷

shoulder ❸

❹ elbow

❺ hair

❻ arm

❼ neck

❽ chest

❾ stomach

❿ leg

⓫ knee

⓬ foot

3 Match and repeat: face

Match the numbered facial features with the list on the right.

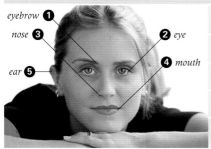

eyebrow ❶

nose ❸

❷ *eye*

❹ *mouth*

ear ❺

1 **la ceja**
   lah <u>thay</u>ah

2 **el ojo**
   el <u>oh</u>-hoh

3 **la nariz**
   lah na<u>reeth</u>

4 **la boca**
   lah <u>bok</u>ah

5 **la oreja**
   lah oh<u>ray</u>ah

4 Useful phrases

Learn these phrases and then test yourself using the cover flap.

*I have a pain in
my back.*

**Tengo un dolor en la
espalda.**
<u>ten</u>goh oon do<u>lor</u> en
lah es<u>pal</u>da

*I have a rash on
my arm.*

**Tengo un sarpullido
en el brazo.**
<u>ten</u>goh oon
sarpoo<u>yee</u>doh en el
<u>brath</u>oh

I don't feel well.

**No me encuentro
bien.**
noh may en<u>kwen</u>troh
byen

5 Put into practice

Join in this conversation and test yourself using the cover flap.

**¿Cuál es el
problema?**
kwal es el pro<u>ble</u>mah
What's the problem?

Say: I don't feel well.

**No me encuentro
bien.**
noh may en<u>kwen</u>troh
byen

¿Dónde le duele?
<u>don</u>day lay <u>dwe</u>lay
Where does it hurt?

*Say: I have a pain in
my shoulder.*

**Tengo un dolor en el
hombro.**
<u>ten</u>goh oon do<u>lor</u> en el
<u>om</u>broh

1 Warm up

Say "I need some tablets." (pp.60–1, pp.88–9)

Say "He needs some cream." (pp.88–9)

What is the Spanish for "I don't have a son"? (pp.10–15)

En el médico
At the doctor

Unless it's an emergency, you have to make an appointment with the doctor and pay when you leave. You may be able to reclaim the money if you have medical insurance. Your hotel, a local pharmacy, or a tourist information office may be able to tell you the names and addresses of local doctors.

2 Useful phrases you may hear

Practice these phrases and then test yourself using the cover flap to conceal the Spanish on the left.

No es grave. noh es <u>gra</u>vay	*It's not serious.*
Necesita hacerse unas pruebas. nethe<u>see</u>tah ah<u>ther</u>say <u>oo</u>nas pr<u>way</u>bas	*You need to have some tests.*
Tiene una infección de riñón. <u>tye</u>nay <u>oo</u>nah infekth<u>yon</u> day rree<u>nyon</u>	*You have a kidney infection.*
Necesita ir al hospital. nethe<u>see</u>tah eer al ospee<u>tal</u>	*You need to go to the hospital.*

Le voy a dar una receta.
lay boy ah dar <u>oo</u>nah rre<u>the</u>tah
I'm going to give you a prescription.

3 In conversation

¿Cuál es el problema?
kwal es el pro<u>ble</u>mah

What's the problem?

Tengo un dolor en el pecho.
<u>ten</u>goh oon do<u>lor</u> en el <u>pe</u>choh

I have a pain in my chest.

Déjeme que la examine.
<u>day</u>haymay kay lah eksa<u>mee</u>nay

Let me examine you.

> **Cultural tip** Before you go to Spain, find out if your health insurance covers emergency medical care in Europe; if it doesn't, purchase a travel medical insurance policy. For an ambulance, call 112.

4 Useful phrases you may need to say

Practice these phrases and then test yourself using the cover flap.

Estoy embarazada.
es<u>toy</u> embar<u>ath</u>adah
I am pregnant.

I am diabetic.	**Soy diabético/-a.** soy deeah<u>be</u>teekoh/-ah
I am epileptic.	**Soy epiléptico/-a.** soy epee<u>lep</u>teekoh/-ah
I have asthma.	**Soy asmático/-a.** soy as<u>ma</u>teekoh/-ah
I have a heart condition.	**Tengo un problema de corazón.** <u>ten</u>goh oon <u>pro</u>blemah day kora<u>thon</u>
I have a temperature.	**Tengo fiebre.** <u>ten</u>goh <u>fyay</u>bray
I feel faint.	**Estoy mareado.** es<u>toy</u> maray-<u>ah</u>doh
It's urgent.	**Es urgente.** es oor<u>hen</u>tay

5 Say it

My son is diabetic.

I have a pain in my arm.

It's not urgent.

¿Es grave?
es <u>gra</u>vay

Is it serious?

No, sólo tiene indigestión.
noh, <u>so</u>loh <u>tye</u>nay indeehesty<u>on</u>

No, you only have indigestion.

¡Menos mal!
<u>may</u>nos mal

What a relief!

1 **Warm up**

Say "How long is the trip?" (pp.42–3)

Ask "Is is serious?" (pp.92–3)

What is the Spanish for "mouth" and "head"? (pp.90–1)

En el hospital
At the hospital

It is useful to know a few basic phrases relating to hospitals and medical treatment for use in an emergency, or in case you need to visit a friend or colleague in the hospital. Most Spanish hospitals have only two beds per room with their own private bathroom facilities.

2 **Useful phrases**

Familiarize yourself with these phrases. Conceal the Spanish with the cover flap and test yourself.

¿Cuáles son las horas de visita? kwales son las oras day beeseetah	*What are the visiting hours?*
¿Cuánto tiempo va a tardar? kwantoh tyempoh bah ah tardar	*How long will it take?*
¿Va a doler? bah ah doler	*Will it hurt?*
Túmbese aquí por favor. toombesay ahkee por fabor	*Please lie down here.*
No puede comer nada. noh pweday komer nadah	*You cannot eat anything.*
No mueva la cabeza. noh mwebah lah kabethah	*Don't move your head.*
Abra la boca por favor. ahbrah lah bokah por fabor	*Please open your mouth.*
Necesita un análisis de sangre. netheseetah oon analeesees day sangray	*You need a blood test.*

el gotero
el goteroh
drip

¿Se encuentra mejor?
say enkwentrah mehor
Are you feeling better?

¿Dónde está la sala de espera?
donday estah lah salah day esperah
Where is the waiting room?

3 Words to remember

Familiarize yourself with these words and test yourself using the flap.

Su radiografía es normal.
soo rradyografeeah es normal
Your X-ray is normal.

emergency room	**el servicio de urgencias**	el ser<u>bee</u>thyoh day oor<u>hen</u>theeas
X-ray department	**el servicio de radiología**	el ser<u>bee</u>thyoh day rradyolo<u>hee</u>ah
children's ward	**la sala de pediatría**	lah <u>sa</u>lah day pedeea<u>tree</u>ah
operating room	**el quirófano**	el kee<u>ro</u>fanoh
waiting room	**la sala de espera**	lah <u>sa</u>lah day es<u>pe</u>rah
stairs	**las escaleras**	las eska<u>le</u>ras

4 Put into practice

Join in this conversation. Cover up the text on the right and complete the answering part of the dialogue in Spanish. Check your answers and repeat if necessary.

Tiene una infección.
<u>tye</u>nay <u>oo</u>nah infekthy<u>on</u>
You have an infection.

Ask: *Do I need tests?*

¿Necesito hacerme pruebas?
neth<u>e</u>seetoh ah<u>ther</u>may pr<u>way</u>bas

Primero necesita un análisis de sangre.
pree<u>me</u>roh neth<u>e</u>seetah oon an<u>a</u>leesees day <u>san</u>gray
First you will need a blood test.

Ask: *Will it hurt?*

¿Me va a doler?
may bah ah do<u>ler</u>

5 Say it

Does he need a blood test?

Where is the children's ward?

Do I need an X-ray?

No, no se preocupe.
noh, noh say pray-o<u>koo</u>pay
No. Don't worry.

Ask: *How long will it take?*

¿Cuánto tiempo va a tardar?
<u>kwan</u>toh <u>tyem</u>poh bah ah tar<u>dar</u>

Repase y repita
Review and repeat

1 The body

1 **la cabeza**
lah ka<u>beth</u>ah

2 **el brazo**
el <u>brath</u>oh

3 **el pecho**
el <u>pech</u>oh

4 **el estómago**
el es<u>tom</u>agoh

5 **la pierna**
lah <u>pyair</u>nah

6 **la rodilla**
lah rro<u>dee</u>yah

7 **el pie**
el pee-<u>ay</u>

1 The body

Name the numbered body parts in Spanish.

1 *head*
2 *arm*
chest 3
4 *stomach*
leg 5
knee 6
foot 7

2 On the phone

1 **Quisiera hablar con Ana Flores.**
kee<u>syair</u>ah hab<u>lar</u> kon <u>ann</u>a <u>flor</u>es

2 **Luis Cortés de Don Frío.**
<u>loo</u>ees kor<u>tes</u> day don <u>free</u>-oh

3 **¿Puedo dejar un mensaje?**
<u>pwe</u>doh de<u>har</u> oon men<u>sah</u>ay

4 **La cita el lunes a las once está bien.**
lah <u>thee</u>tah el <u>loo</u>nes ah las <u>on</u>thay es<u>tah</u> byen

5 **Gracias, adiós.**
<u>grath</u>yas, addy-<u>os</u>

2 On the phone

You are arranging an appointment. Follow the conversation, replying in Spanish following the English prompts.

Dígame, Apex Finanzas.
1 *I'd like to speak to Ana Flores.*

¿De parte de quién?
2 *Luis Cortés, of Don Frío.*

Lo siento, está comunicando.
3 *Can I leave a message?*

Sí, dígame.
4 *The appointment on Monday at 11 am is fine.*

Muy bien, adiós.
5 *Thank you, goodbye.*

3 Clothing

Say the Spanish words for the numbered items of clothing.

tie **1**

jacket **2**

pants **3**

4 *skirt*

shoes **5**

pantyhose **6**

3 Clothing

1 **la corbata**
lah kor<u>ba</u>tah

2 **la chaqueta**
lah cha<u>ke</u>tah

3 **el pantalón**
el panta<u>lon</u>

4 **la falda**
lah <u>fal</u>dah

5 **los zapatos**
los tha<u>pa</u>tos

6 **las medias**
las <u>me</u>deeas

4 At the doctor's

Say these phrases in Spanish.

1 *I don't feel well.*

2 *I have a heart condition.*

3 *Do I need to go to the hospital?*

4 *I'm pregnant.*

4 At the doctor's

1 **No me encuentro bien.**
noh may en<u>kwen</u>troh byen

2 **Tengo un problema de corazón.**
<u>ten</u>goh oon pro<u>ble</u>mah day kora<u>thon</u>

3 **¿Necesito ir al hospital?**
nethe<u>see</u>toh eer al ospee<u>tal</u>

4 **Estoy embarazada.**
es<u>toy</u> embara<u>tha</u>dah

1 Warm up

Say the months of the year in Spanish. (pp.28–9)

Ask "Is there a parking lot?" and "Are there restrooms?" (pp.48–9 and pp.62-3)

En casa
At home

Many city-dwellers live in apartment blocks (**edificios**), but in rural areas the houses tend to be single-family (**chalet**). If you want to know how big it is, you will need to ask in square meters. If you want to know how many bedrooms there are, ask **¿Cuántos dormitorios hay?**.

2 Match and repeat

Match the numbered items to the list and test yourself using the flap.

1 **la chimenea**
lah cheemenayah

2 **la ventana**
lah bentanah

3 **el tejado**
el tehadoh

4 **la terraza**
lah terratha

5 **la persiana**
lah perseeanah

6 **el muro**
el mooroh

7 **la puerta**
lah pwertah

8 **el garaje**
el garahay

❶ *chimney*

❷ *window*

❻ *wall*

❺ *shutters*

Cultural tip You almost never see a Spanish home without shutters at every window. These are closed at night and often during the heat of the day in summer. Drapes, where they exist at all, tend to be more for decoration. Carpets are not popular in Spanish homes; ceramic tiles or parquet floors with rugs are a more common flooring solution.

3 Words to remember

Familiarize yourself with these words and test yourself using the flap.

¿Cuánto es el alquiler al mes?
kwantoh es el alkeeler al mes
What is the rent per month?

room	**la habitación** lah abeetathyon
floor	**el suelo** el sweloh
ceiling	**el techo** el techoh
bedroom	**el dormitorio** el dormeetoreeoh
bathroom	**el cuarto de baño** el kwartoh day banyoh
kitchen	**la cocina** lah kotheenah
dining room	**el comedor** el komedor
living room	**el cuarto de estar** el kwartoh day estar
basement	**el sótano** el sotahnoh
attic	**el ático** el ahteekoh

3 *roof*

4 *terrace*

8 *garage*

7 *door*

4 Useful phrases

Practice these phrases and test yourself.

¿Hay un garaje?
ah-ee oon garahay

Is there a garage?

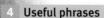

¿Cuándo está disponible?
kwandoh estah deesponeeblay

When is it available?

MAY MAI MAI MEI

5 Say it

Is there a dining room?

Is it large?

Is it available in July?

¿Está amueblado?
estah amwebladoh

Is it furnished?

En la casa
Inside the house

If you're renting a vacation house or villa in Spain, the most common option is to take it for a full month or, if not, for a **quincena**, the first or last fifteen days of the month. You will need to check in advance whether the cost of utilities is included in the rent. Most vacation homes have no telephone.

2 Match and repeat

Match the numbered items to the list in the panel on the left. Then test yourself by concealing the Spanish with the cover flap.

1 **la encimera**
lah entheemerah

2 **el fregadero**
el fregaderoh

3 **el microondas**
el meekro-ondas

4 **el horno**
el ornoh

5 **la cocina**
lah kotheenah

6 **el frigorífico**
el freegoreefeekoh

7 **la mesa**
lah mesah

8 **la silla**
lah seeyah

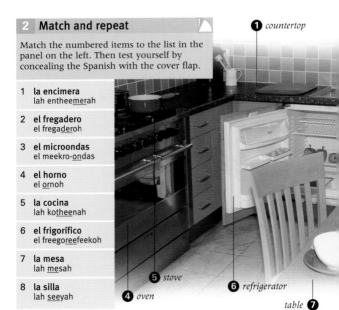

❶ countertop

❺ stove

❹ oven

❻ refrigerator

table ❼

3 In conversation

Este es el horno.
estay es el ornoh

This is the oven.

¿Hay también un lavavajillas?
ah-ee tambyen oon lababaheeyas

Is there a dishwasher as well?

Sí, y hay un congelador grande.
see, ee ah-ee oon konhelador granday

Yes, and there's a big freezer.

4 Words to remember

Familiarize yourself with these words and test yourself using the flap.

wardrobe	**el armario**	el ar<u>mar</u>yoh
sofa	**el sofá**	el so<u>fah</u>
fireplace	**la chimenea**	lah cheeme<u>nay</u>ah
carpet	**la moqueta**	lah mo<u>ket</u>ah
bathtub	**la bañera**	lah ban<u>yer</u>ah
toilet	**el váter**	el <u>bat</u>er
bathroom sink	**el lavabo**	el <u>lab</u>aboh

El sofá es nuevo.
el so<u>fah</u> es <u>nwe</u>boh
The sofa is new.

microwave ❸

❷ sink

❽ chair

5 Useful phrases

Practice these phrases and then test yourself.

The stove is broken.	**La cocina no funciona.** lah ko<u>thee</u>nah noh foonth<u>yon</u>ah
I don't like the drapes.	**No me gustan las cortinas.** noh may <u>goo</u>stan las kor<u>teen</u>as
Is electricity included?	**¿Está incluida la electricidad?** es<u>tah</u> eenkloo<u>ee</u>dah lah ehektreethee<u>dad</u>

6 Say it

Is there a microwave?

I like the fireplace.

What a soft sofa!

Todo está muy nuevo.
<u>to</u>doh es<u>tah</u> mwee <u>nwe</u>boh

Everything is very new.

Y aquí está la lavadora.
ee ah<u>kee</u> es<u>tah</u> lah laba<u>dor</u>ah

And here's the washing machine.

¡Qué azulejos más bonitos!
kay ah-thoo<u>lay</u>hos mas bo<u>nee</u>tos

What beautiful tiles!

Say "I need" and "you need." (pp.64-5, pp.92-4)

What is the Spanish for "day" and "month"? (pp.28-9)

Say the days of the week. (pp.28-9)

El jardín
The backyard

The yard of a house or villa may be communal, or at least partly shared. Check with the realtor or rental agent carefully to find out. In some cases, a charge for maintenance of the yard may be included with the rent of an apartment or house. Check such details with the agent.

2 Words to remember

Familiarize yourself with these words and test yourself using the flap.

la máquina cortacésped lah <u>ma</u>keenah korta<u>thes</u>ped	*lawnmower*
la horca lah <u>or</u>kah	*fork*
la pala lah <u>pa</u>lah	*spade*
el rastrillo el rras<u>tree</u>yoh	*rake*
el vivero el bee<u>be</u>roh	*garden center*

❷ *tree*

❸ *soil*

terrace ❶

flowers ❼   *weeds* ❽   ❾ *path*

3 Useful phrases

Practice these phrases and then test yourself using the cover flap.

	The gardener comes once a week.	**El jardinero viene una vez a la semana.** el hardee<u>nair</u>oh <u>bya</u>inay <u>oo</u>nah beth ah lah se<u>ma</u>nah
	Can you mow the lawn?	**¿Puede cortar el césped?** <u>pwe</u>day kor<u>tar</u> el <u>thes</u>ped
	Is the yard private?	**¿Es el jardín privado?** es el har<u>deen</u> pree<u>ba</u>doh
	The garden needs watering.	**El jardín necesita que lo rieguen.** el har<u>deen</u> nethe<u>see</u>tah kay loh <u>rree</u>ayghen

4 Match and repeat

Match the numbered items to the words in the panel on the right.

❹ *lawn* ❺ *hedge* ❻ *plants*

flowerbed ❿

1 **la terraza**
  lah te<u>rra</u>thah

2 **el árbol**
  el <u>ar</u>bol

3 **la tierra**
  lah <u>tya</u>irrah

4 **el césped**
  el <u>thes</u>ped

5 **el seto**
  el <u>se</u>toh

6 **las plantas**
  las <u>plan</u>tas

7 **las flores**
  las <u>flo</u>res

8 **las malas hierbas**
  las <u>ma</u>las <u>yer</u>bas

9 **el camino**
  el ka<u>mee</u>noh

10 **el parterre**
  el par<u>tai</u>rray

5 Say it

The lawn needs water.

Are there any trees?

The gardener comes on Fridays.

1 Warm up

Say "My name is ...".
(pp.8–9)

Say "Don't worry."
(pp.94–5)

What is "your" in
Spanish? (pp.12–13)

Los animales de compañía
Pets

Many Spanish families have pets—
dogs are especially popular—and
veterinary services are generally good.
Ask your vet about the necessary
paperwork if you are considering
traveling to Spain with your pet.

2 Match and repeat

Match the numbered animals to the Spanish
words in the panel on the left. Then test yourself
using the cover flap.

1 **el gato**
el gatoh

2 **el conejo**
el konehoh

3 **el pájaro**
el paharoh

4 **el pez**
el peth

5 **el perro**
el perroh

6 **el hámster**
el hamster

bird ❸

❷ *rabbit*

❶ *cat*

fish ❹

dog ❺

❻ *hamster*

3 Useful phrases

Learn these phrases and then test yourself using
the cover flap.

¿Es bueno el perro? es bwenoh el perroh	*Is this dog friendly?*
¿Puedo llevar el perro? pwedoh yebar el perroh	*Can I bring my dog?*
Me dan miedo los gatos. may dan myaydoh los gatos	*I'm afraid of cats.*
Mi perro no muerde. mee perroh noh mweday	*My dog doesn't bite.*

Este gato está lleno de pulgas.
estay gatoh estah yenoh day poolgas
This cat is full of fleas.

Cultural tip Many dogs in Spain are working or guard dogs, and you may encounter them tethered or roaming free. Approach farms and rural houses with particular care. Look out for warning notices such as "¡Cuidado con el perro!" (Beware of the dog).

4 Words to remember

Familiarize yourself with these words and test yourself using the flap.

Mi perro no está bien.
mee perroh noh estah
byen
My dog is not well.

basket	**la cesta**	lah thestah
cage	**la jaula**	lah haoolah
bowl	**el bol**	el bol
collar	**el collar**	el koyar
leash	**la correa**	lah korray-ah
vet	**el veterinario**	el betereenaryoh
vaccination	**la vacuna**	lah bakoonah
pet passport	**el pasaporte de animales**	el pasaportay day aneemales
flea spray	**el spray antipulgas**	el espraee anteepoolgas

5 Put into practice

Join in this conversation. Read the Spanish on the left and follow the instructions to make your reply. Then test yourself by concealing the answers with the cover flap.

¿Es suyo este perro?
es sooyoh estay perroh
Is this your dog?

Say: Yes, his name is Sandy.

Sí, se llama Sandy.
see, say yamah Sandy

Me dan miedo los perros.
may dan myaydoh los perros
I'm afraid of dogs.

Say: Don't worry. He's friendly.

No se preocupe. Es bueno.
noh say prayohkoopay. es bwenoh

Repase y repita
Review and repeat

1 Colors

1 Colors

1 **negra**
<u>neg</u>rah

2 **pequeños**
pe<u>ken</u>yos

3 **rojo**
<u>rro</u>hoh

4 **verde**
<u>ber</u>day

5 **amarillos**
ama<u>ree</u>yos

Complete the sentences with the Spanish word for the color in brackets. Watch out for masculine and feminine.

1 Quisiera la camisa ____. (black)

2 Estos zapatos son muy ____. (small)

3 ¿Tiene este traje en ____ ? (red)

4 No, pero lo tengo en ____. (green)

5 Quiero los zapatos ____. (yellow)

2 Kitchen

2 Kitchen

1 **la cocina**
lah ko<u>thee</u>nah

2 **el frigorífico**
el freego<u>ree</u>feekoh

3 **el fregadero**
el frega<u>de</u>roh

4 **el microondas**
el meekro-<u>on</u>das

5 **el horno**
el <u>or</u>noh

6 **la silla**
lah <u>see</u>yah

7 **la mesa**
lah <u>me</u>sah

Say the Spanish words for the numbered items.

1 stove   refrigerator 2

oven 5   chair 6

3 House

You are visiting a house in Spain. Join in the conversation, asking questions in Spanish following the English prompts.

Éste es el cuarto de estar.
1 *What a lovely fireplace.*

Sí, y tiene una cocina muy grande.
2 *How many bedrooms are there?*

Hay tres dormitorios.
3 *Do you have a garage?*

Sí, pero no hay un jardín.
4 *When is it available?*

En julio.
5 *What is the rent per month?*

3 House

1 **¡Qué chimenea más bonita!**
kay cheemenayah mas boneetah

2 **¿Cuántos dormitorios hay?**
kwantos dormeetoreeos ah-ee

3 **¿Tiene garaje?**
tyenay garahay

4 **¿Cuándo está disponible?**
kwandoh estah deesponeeblay

5 **¿Cuánto es el alquiler al mes?**
kwantoh es el alkeeler al mes

microwave ❹

❸ *sink*

table ❼

4 At home

Say the Spanish for the following items.

1 *washing machine*

2 *sofa*

3 *attic*

4 *dining room*

5 *tree*

6 *garden*

4 At home

1 **la lavadora**
lah labadorah

2 **el sofá**
el sofah

3 **el ático**
el ahteekoh

4 **el comedor**
el komedor

5 **el árbol**
el arbol

6 **el jardín**
el hardeen

1 Warm up

Ask "How do I get to the bank?" and "How do I get to the post office?" (pp.50–1)

What's the Spanish for "passport"? (pp.54–5)

How do you ask "What time is the meeting?" (pp.30–1)

El banco y la oficina de correos
Bank and post office

Banks and post offices usually open only until lunchtime (approximately 2 pm) and are generally closed on weekends. **Cajas de ahorros** (savings banks) have different hours. In the summer, opening times may be shorter.

2 Words to remember: mail

Familiarize yourself with these words and test yourself using the cover flap to conceal the Spanish on the left.

los sellos los <u>se</u>yos	*stamps*
la postal lah pos<u>tal</u>	*postcard*
el paquete el pa<u>ke</u>tay	*package*
por avión por ab<u>yon</u>	*by air mail*
el correo certificado el ko<u>rray</u>oh therteefee<u>ka</u>doh	*registered mail*
el buzón el boo<u>thon</u>	*mailbox*
el código postal el <u>ko</u>deegoh postal	*postal (ZIP) code*
el cartero el kar<u>tair</u>oh	*mail carrier*

¿Cuánto es para el Reino Unido?
<u>kwan</u>toh es <u>pa</u>rah el <u>rray</u>eenoh oo<u>nee</u>doh
How much is it to the United Kingdom?

el sobre
el <u>so</u>bray
envelope

3 In conversation

Quisiera sacar dinero.
kee<u>syai</u>rah sa<u>kar</u> dee<u>ne</u>roh

I'd like to withdraw some money.

¿Tiene identificación?
<u>tye</u>nay eedenteefeekath<u>yon</u>

Do you have any ID?

Sí, aquí tiene mi pasaporte.
see, ah<u>kee tye</u>nay mee pasa<u>por</u>tay

Yes, here's my passport.

4 Words to remember: bank

Familiarize yourself with these words and test yourself using the flap to cover the Spanish on the right.

	PIN	**el pin** el peen
	bank	**el banco** el <u>ban</u>koh
	teller	**el cajero** el ka<u>he</u>roh
	ATM	**el cajero automático** el ka<u>he</u>roh aooto<u>ma</u>teekoh
	notes (bills)	**los billetes** los bee<u>ye</u>tes
	traveler's checks	**los cheques de viaje** los <u>che</u>kes day <u>bee</u>ahay

¿Cómo puedo pagar?
<u>ko</u>moh <u>pwe</u>doh pagar
How can I pay?

5 Useful phrases

Practice these phrases and then test yourself using the cover flap.

6 Say it

I'd like to change some traveler's checks.

Do I need my passport?

How much is it for a postcard.

I'd like to change some money.	**Quisiera cambiar dinero.** kee<u>sy</u>airah kamb<u>yar</u> dee<u>ne</u>roh
What is the exchange rate?	**¿A cuánto está el cambio?** ah <u>kwan</u>toh es<u>tah</u> el <u>kam</u>byoh
I'd like to withdraw some money.	**Quisiera sacar dinero.** kee<u>sy</u>airah sa<u>kar</u> dee<u>ne</u>roh

Meta su pin, por favor.
<u>me</u>tah soo peen, por fa<u>bor</u>

Please type in your PIN.

¿Tengo que firmar también?
<u>ten</u>goh kay fee<u>rmar</u> tamb<u>yen</u>

Do I have to sign, too?

No, no hace falta.
noh, noh <u>ah</u>thay <u>fal</u>tah

No, that's not necessary.

1 Warm up

What is the Spanish for "doesn't work"? (pp.60–1)

What's the Spanish for "today" and "tomorrow"? (pp.28–9)

Los servicios
Services

You can combine the Spanish words on these pages with the vocabulary you learned in week 10 to help you explain basic problems and cope with arranging most repairs. When negotiating building work or a repair, it's a good idea to agree on the price and method of payment in advance.

2 Words to remember

Familiarize yourself with these words and test yourself using the flap.

el fontanero el fonta*nair*oh	*plumber*
el electricista el ehlektree*thees*tah	*electrician*
el mecánico el me*kan*eekoh	*mechanic*
el albañil el alban*yeel*	*handyman*
la asistenta lah asee*sten*tah	*cleaner*
el pintor el peen*tor*	*decorator*
el carpintero el karpeen*ter*oh	*carpenter*
el técnico el *tek*neekoh	*technician*

la llave de tuercas
lah *yab*ay day *twer*kas
tire iron

No necesito un mecánico.
noh nethe*see*toh oon me*kan*eekoh
I don't need a mechanic.

3 In conversation

La lavadora no funciona.
lah laba*dor*ah noh foothyo*nah*

The washing machine's not working.

Sí, la manguera está rota.
see, lah man*gher*ah estah *rrot*ah

Yes, the hose is broken.

¿La puede arreglar?
lah *pwed*ay arreg*lar*

Can you repair it?

4 Useful phrases

Practice these phrases and then test yourself using the cover flap.

¿Dónde me pueden arreglar la plancha?
donday may pweden arreglar lah planchah
Where can I get the iron repaired?

Can you clean the bathroom?	**¿Puede limpiar el cuarto de baño?** pweday leempyar el kwartoh day banyoh
Can you repair the boiler?	**¿Puede arreglar la caldera?** pweday arreglar lah kalderah
Do you know a good electrician?	**¿Conoce a un buen electricista?** konothay ah oon bwen ehlektreetheestah

5 Put into practice

Practice these phrases. Cover up the text on the right and complete the dialogue in Spanish. Check your answers and repeat if necessary.

los planos
los planos
plans

Empiezo el trabajo mañana.
empyaythoh el trabahoh manyanah
I start the job tomorrow.

Su verja está rota.
soo berhah estah rrotah
Your gate is broken.

Ask: Do you know a good handyman?

¿Conoce a un buen albañil?
konothay ah oon bwen albanyeel

Sí, hay uno en el pueblo.
see, ah-ee oonoh en el pwebloh
Yes, there is one in the village.

Ask: Do you have his phone number?

¿Tiene su número de teléfono?
tyenay soo noomeroh day telefonoh

No, va a necesitar una nueva.
noh, bah ah netheseetar oonah nwebah

No, you'll need a new one.

¿Lo puede hacer hoy?
loh pweday ahther oy

Can you do it today?

No, volveré mañana.
noh, bolberay manyanah

No. I'll come back tomorrow.

Venir
To come

The verb **venir** (*to come*) is one of the most useful verbs. As well as the main verb (see below) it is worth knowing the command **¡ven!/¡venga!** (come here! informal/formal). Note that *with me* becomes **conmigo** and *with you* **contigo**: **ven conmigo** (*come with me*); **vengo contigo** (*I'm going with you*).

2 Venir: to come

Say the different forms of the verb aloud, reading from the table. Use the cover flaps to test yourself and, when you are confident, practice the sample sentences listed below.

yo vengo yoh <u>ben</u>goh	*I come*
tú vienes/usted viene too <u>bye</u>nes/<u>oos</u>ted <u>bye</u>nay	*you come (informal/ formal singular)*
él/ella viene el/<u>eh</u>-yah <u>bye</u>nay	*he/she comes*
nosotros(-as) venimos no<u>so</u>tros(-as) ben<u>ee</u>mos	*we come*
vosotros(-as) venís bo<u>so</u>tros(-as) ben<u>ee</u>s	*you come (informal plural)*
ustedes vienen oos<u>te</u>des <u>bye</u>nen	*you come (formal plural)*
ellos/ellas vienen <u>eh</u>-yos/<u>eh</u>-yas <u>bye</u>nen	*they come*
Vengo ahora. <u>ben</u>goh ah-<u>or</u>ah	*I'm coming now.*
Venimos todos los martes. ben<u>ee</u>mos <u>to</u>dos los <u>mar</u>tes	*We come every Tuesday.*
Vienen en tren. <u>bye</u>nen en tren	*They come by train.*

Vienen en muchos colores.
bee<u>ay</u>nen en <u>moo</u>chos <u>ko</u>lores
They come in many colors.

Conversational tip To say "I come from the US" in Spanish, you have to use the verb "to be," as in "soy estadounidense" (I am from the US). When you use the verb "to come," as in "Vengo de Nueva York," it means you have just arrived from New York.

3 Useful phrases

Learn these phrases and then test yourself using the cover flap.

When can I come?	**¿Cuándo puedo venir?** kwandoh pwedoh beneer
Does it come in size 44?	**¿Viene en la talla 44?** byenay en lah tayah kwarentah ee kwatroh
The cleaner comes every Monday.	**La asistenta viene todos los lunes.** lah aseestentah byenay todos los loones

¿Puede venir el viernes?
pweday beneer el byairnes
Can you come on Friday?

Come with me. (informal/formal)	**Ven conmigo/ Venga conmigo.** ben konmeegoh/ bengah konmeegoh

4 Put into practice

Practice these phrases. Then cover up the text on the right and say the anwering part of the dialogue in Spanish. Check your answers and repeat if necessary.

Peluquería Cristina, dígame.
pelookereeah kristeenah, deegamay
Christine's hair salon. Can I help you?

Say: I'd like an appointment.

Quisiera una cita.
keesyairah oonah theetah

¿Cuándo quiere venir?
kwandoh kyairay beneer
When do you want to come?

Say: Today, if possible.

Hoy, si es posible.
oy, see es poseeblay

Sí, claro. ¿A qué hora?
see klaroh, ah kay orah
Yes, of course. What time?

Say: At 10:30.

A las diez y media.
ah las dyeth ee medeeah

What's the Spanish for "big" and "small"? (pp.64–5)

Say "The room is big" and "The bed is small." (pp.64–5)

La policía y el delito
Police and crime

While in Spain, if you are the victim of a crime, you should go to the police station to report it, or in an emergency you can dial 112. You may have to explain your complaint in Spanish, so some basic vocabulary is useful.

2 Words to remember: crime

Familiarize yourself with these words.

el robo el rroboh	*robbery*
la denuncia lah denoontheeah	*police report*
el ladrón el ladron	*thief*
la policía lah poleetheeah	*police*
la declaración lah deklarathyon	*statement*
el testigo el testeegoh	*witness*
el abogado el abogadoh	*lawyer*

Necesito un abogado.
netheseetoh oon abogadoh
I need a lawyer.

3 Useful phrases

Learn these phrases and then test yourself.

Me han robado. may an rrobadoh	*I've been robbed.*
¿Qué han robado? kay an rrobadoh	*What was stolen?*
¿Vió quién lo hizo? byoh kyain loh eethoh	*Did you see who did it?*
¿Cuándo ocurrió? kwandoh okoorryoh	*When did it happen?*

la cámara de fotos
lah kamarah day fotos
camera

la cartera
la karterah
wallet

4 Words to remember: appearance

Learn these words. Remember, some adjectives have a feminine form.

Él es bajo y tiene bigote.
el es <u>ba</u>hoh ee <u>tye</u>nay bee<u>go</u>tay
He is short and has a mustache.

Tiene el pelo negro y corto.
<u>tye</u>nay el <u>pe</u>loh <u>ne</u>groh ee <u>kor</u>toh
He has short, black hair.

man	**el hombre** el <u>om</u>bray	
woman	**la mujer** lah moo-<u>hair</u>	
tall	**alto/alta** <u>al</u>toh/<u>al</u>tah	
short	**bajo/baja** <u>ba</u>hoh/<u>ba</u>hah	
young	**joven** <u>ho</u>ben	
old	**viejo/vieja** <u>bye</u>yhoh/<u>bye</u>yhah	
fat	**gordo/gorda** <u>gor</u>doh/<u>gor</u>dah	
thin	**delgado/delgada** del<u>ga</u>doh/del<u>ga</u>dah	
long/short hair	**el pelo largo/corto** el <u>pe</u>loh <u>lar</u>goh/<u>kor</u>toh	
glasses	**las gafas** las <u>ga</u>fas	
beard	**la barba** la <u>bar</u>bah	

Cultural tip In Spain there is a difference between la guardia civil and la policía. La policía are the local police while la guardia civil operates in airports and patrols the national road system. The police uniforms are blue and those of the guardia civil are green.

5 Put into practice

Practice these phrases. Then cover up the text on the right and follow the instructions to make your reply in Spanish.

¿Cómo era?
<u>ko</u>moh <u>eh</u>rah
What did he look like?

Say: Short and fat.

Bajo y gordo.
<u>ba</u>hoh ee <u>gor</u>doh

¿Y el pelo?
ee el <u>pe</u>loh
And his hair?

Say: Long, with a beard.

Largo y con barba.
<u>lar</u>goh ee kon <u>bar</u>bah

Respuestas
Answers
Cover with flap

Repase y repita
Review and repeat

1 To come

1 **vienen**
byenen

2 **viene**
byenay

3 **venimos**
beneemos

4 **venís**
benees

5 **vengo**
bengoh

1 To come

Fill in the blanks with the correct form of **venir** (*to come*).

1 Mis padres ____ a las cuatro.

2 La asistenta ____ una vez a la semana.

3 Nosotros ____ todos los martes.

4 ¿ ____ vosotros con nosotros?

5 Yo ____ en taxi.

2 Bank and mail

1 **los billetes**
los beeyetes

2 **la postal**
lah postal

3 **el paquete**
el paketay

4 **el sobre**
el sobray

2 Bank and mail

Name these items.

❶ *bills (notes)*

❷ *postcard*

❸ *package*

envelope ❹

3 Appearance

What do these descriptions mean?

1 **Es un hombre alto y delgado.**

2 **Ella tiene el pelo corto y gafas.**

3 **Soy baja y tengo el pelo largo.**

4 **Ella es vieja y gorda.**

5 **Él tiene los ojos azules y barba.**

3 Appearance

1 *He's a tall, thin man.*

2 *She has short hair and glasses.*

3 *I'm short and I have long hair.*

4 *She's old and fat.*

5 *He has blue eyes and a beard.*

4 The pharmacy

You are asking a pharmacist for advice. Join in the conversation, replying in Spanish following the English prompts.

Buenos días, ¿qué desea?
1 *I have a cough.*

¿Le duele el pecho?
2 *No, but I have a headache.*

Tiene estas pastillas.
3 *Do you have that as a syrup?*

Sí señor. Aquí tiene.
4 *Thank you. How much is that?*

Cuatro euros.
5 *Here you are. Goodbye.*

4 The pharmacy

1 **Tengo tos.**
   <u>ten</u>goh tos

2 **No, pero me duele la cabeza.**
   noh, <u>pe</u>roh may <u>dwe</u>lay lah ka<u>be</u>thah

3 **¿Lo tiene en jarabe?**
   loh <u>tye</u>nay en ha<u>ra</u>bay

4 **Gracias. ¿Cuánto es?**
   <u>gra</u>thyas. <u>kwan</u>toh es

5 **Aquí tiene. Adiós.**
   ah<u>kee tye</u>nay. addy-<u>os</u>

1 Warm up

What is the Spanish for "museum" and "art gallery"? (pp.48–9)

Say "I don't like the curtains." (pp.100–1)

Ask "Do you want…?" informally. (pp.22–3)

El ocio
Leisure time

The Spanish pride themselves on their lively nightlife and support for the arts, including theater and movies. It is not unusual for Spaniards to number politics or philosophy among their interests. Be prepared for these topics to be the subject of conversation in social situations.

2 Words to remember

Familiarize yourself with these words and test yourself using the cover flap to conceal the Spanish on the left.

el teatro el te-ahtroh	*theater*
el cine el theenay	*movie theater*
la discoteca lah deeskotekah	*discotheque*
el deporte el deportay	*sports*
el turismo el tooreesmoh	*sightseeing*
la política la poleeteekah	*politics*
la música lah mooseekah	*music*
el arte el artay	*art*

Me encanta el baile.
me enkantah el baeelay
I love dancing.

3 In conversation

Hola. ¿Quieres jugar al tenis hoy?
o-lah. kyaires hoogar al tenis oy

Hi, do you want to play tennis today?

No, no me gusta el deporte.
noh, noh may goostah el deportay

No, I don't like sports.

Y entonces, ¿qué te gusta?
ee entonthes, kay tay goostah

So then, what do you like?

4 Useful phrases

Learn these phrases and then test yourself using the cover flap.

los video-juegos
los <u>bee</u>dayoh-<u>hwe</u>gos
video games

la bailadora
lah baeela-<u>do</u>rah
dancer

What are your (formal/informal) interests?	**¿Cuáles son sus/tus intereses?** <u>kwa</u>les son soos/toos inte<u>re</u>ses
I like the theater.	**Me gusta el teatro.** may <u>goos</u>tah el te-<u>ah</u>troh
I prefer the movies.	**Yo prefiero el cine.** yoh pref<u>yai</u>roh el <u>thee</u>nay
I'm interested in art.	**Me interesa el arte.** may inte<u>re</u>sah el <u>ar</u>tay
That bores me.	**Eso me aburre.** <u>eh</u>soh may a<u>boor</u>ray

el traje típico
el <u>tra</u>hay <u>tee</u>peekoh
traditional costume

5 Say it

I'm interested in music.

I prefer sports.

I don't like video games.

Prefiero el turismo e ir de compras.
pref<u>yai</u>roh el too<u>rees</u>moh eh eer day <u>kom</u>pras

I prefer sightseeing and shopping.

Eso a mí no me interesa.
<u>eh</u>soh ah mee noh may inte<u>re</u>sah

That doesn't interest me.

No pasa nada. Me voy yo sola.
noh <u>pa</u>sah <u>na</u>dah. may boy yoh <u>so</u>lah

No problem. I'll go on my own.

1 Warm up

Ask "Do you (formal) want to play tennis?" (pp.118–19)

Say "I like the theater" and "I prefer sightseeing." (pp.118–19)

Say "That doesn't interest me." (pp.118–19)

El deporte y los pasatiempos
Sports and hobbies

Hacer (*to do* or *to make*) and **jugar** (*to play*) are the verbs used most when talking about sports and pastimes. **Jugar** is followed by **a** when you are talking about playing a sport, as in **juego al baloncesto** (*I play basketball*).

2 Words to remember

Familiarize yourself with these words and then test yourself.

el fútbol/rugby el <u>foot</u>bol/<u>roog</u>bee	*soccer/rugby*
el tenis/baloncesto el <u>ten</u>is/balon<u>thes</u>toh	*tennis/basketball*
la natación lah natath<u>yon</u>	*swimming*
la vela lah <u>be</u>lah	*sailing*
la pesca lah <u>pes</u>kah	*fishing*
la pintura lah peen<u>too</u>rah	*painting*
el ciclismo el thee<u>klees</u>moh	*cycling*
el senderismo el sende<u>rees</u>moh	*hiking*

el búnker
 el <u>bun</u>ker
 bunker

el jugador de golf
 el <u>hu</u>gador <br> day golf
 golfer

Juego al golf todos los días.
 <u>hwe</u>goh al golf todos los <u>dee</u>yas
 I play golf every day.

3 Useful phrases

Learn these phrases and then test yourself.

Juego al fútbol. <u>hwe</u>goh al <u>foot</u>bol	*I play soccer.*
Juega al tenis. <u>hwe</u>gah al <u>ten</u>is	*He plays tennis.*
Ella pinta. <u>eh</u>-yah <u>peen</u>tah	*She paints.*

4 Hacer: to do or to make

Hacer is a useful verb meaning "to do" or "to make." It is commonly used to describe leisure pursuits. **Hace** is also used to describe the weather.

I do	**yo hago** yoh ahgoh
you do *(informal/formal* *singular)*	**tú haces/usted hace** too ahthes/oosted ahthay
he/she does	**él/ella hace** el/eh-yah ahthay
we do	**nosotros(-as) hacemos** nosotros(-as) ahthemos
you do (informal *plural)*	**vosotros(-as) hacéis** bosotros(-as) ahthays
you do (formal *plural)*	**ustedes hacen** oostedes ahthen
they do	**ellos/ellas hacen** eh-yos/eh-yas ahthen
What do you like *doing?* *(informal/formal* *singular)*	**¿Qué te/le gusta hacer?** kay tay/lay goostah ahthair?
I go hiking.	**Yo hago senderismo.** yoh ahgoh sendereesmoh

Hoy hace bueno.
oy ahthay bwenoh
It's nice (weather)
today.

la banderola
lah bandairolah
flag

el campo de golf
el kampoh day golf
golf course

5 Put into practice

Join in this conversation following the English prompts.

¿Qué te gusta hacer? kay tay goostah ahthair *What do you like* *doing?* *Say: I like playing* *tennis.*	**Me gusta jugar al tenis.** may goostah hoogar al tenis
¿Juegas al fútbol también? hwegas al footbol tambyen *Do you play soccer,* *too?* *Say: No, I play rugby.*	**No, juego al rugby.** noh, hwegoh al roogbee
¿Cuándo juegas? kwandoh hweges *When do you play?* *Say: I play every* *week.*	**Juego todas las semanas.** hwegoh todas las semanas

Say "my husband"
and "my wife."
(pp.10–11)

Say the days of the
week in Spanish.
(pp.28–9)

Say "Sorry, I'm busy."
(pp.32–3)

La vida social
Socializing

The Spanish dinner table is the center
of the social world. You can expect
to do a lot of your socializing around
the table, enjoying food and wine. In
general, it is best to use the more polite
usted form to talk to older people and
tú with the younger crowd.

2 Useful phrases

Practice these phrases and then test yourself.

Me gustaría invitarte a cenar. may goostar<u>ee</u>ah inbee<u>tar</u>tay ah the<u>nar</u>	*I'd like to invite you to dinner.*
¿Estás libre el miércoles que viene? estas <u>lee</u>bray el m<u>yair</u>koles kay <u>bye</u>nay	*Are you free next Wednesday?*
Quizá otro día. kee<u>thah</u> <u>oh</u>troh <u>dee</u>yah	*Maybe another day.*

Cultural tip When you visit someone's house for the
first time, it is customary to bring flowers or wine. If you
are invited again, having seen your host's house, you can
bring something a little more personal.

3 In conversation

¿Quieres venir a comer el martes?
k<u>yai</u>res ben<u>eer</u> ah ko<u>mer</u> el <u>mar</u>tes

Would you like to come to lunch on Tuesday?

Lo siento, estoy ocupada.
loh s<u>yain</u>toh, es<u>toy</u> okoo<u>pa</u>dah

I'm sorry, I'm busy.

¿Qué tal el jueves?
kay tal el <u>hwe</u>bes

What about Thursday?

4 Words to remember

Familiarize yourself with these words and test yourself using the flap.

la invitada
lah inbee<u>ta</u>dah
guest

la anfitriona
lah anfeetr<u>yo</u>nah
hostess

party	**la fiesta** lah f<u>yay</u>stah	
dinner party	**la cena** lah <u>the</u>nah	
invitation	**la invitación** lah inbeetath<u>yon</u>	
reception	**la recepción** lah rrethepth<u>yon</u>	
cocktail party	**el coctel** el kok<u>tel</u>	

5 Put into practice

Join this conversation, replying in Spanish.

¿Puede venir a una recepción esta noche?
<u>pwe</u>day be<u>neer</u> ah <u>oo</u>nah rrethepth<u>yon</u> <u>es</u>tah <u>no</u>chay
Can you come to a reception tonight?

Say: Yes, I'd love to.

Sí, encantado/-a.
see, enkan-<u>ta</u>doh/-ah

Empieza a las ocho.
emp<u>yay</u>thah ah las <u>o</u>choh
It starts at eight o'clock.

Ask: What should I wear?

¿Qué me pongo?
kay may <u>pon</u>goh

Gracias por invitarnos.
<u>gra</u>thyas por inbee<u>tar</u>nos
Thank you for inviting us.

Encantada.
enkan-<u>ta</u>dah

I'd be delighted.

Ven con tu marido.
ben kon too ma<u>ree</u>doh

Bring your husband.

Gracias, ¿a qué hora?
<u>gra</u>thyas, ah kay <u>o</u>rah

Thank you. What time?

Repase y repita
Review and repeat

1 Animals

1 **el pez**
el peth

2 **el pájaro**
el paharoh

3 **el conejo**
el konehoh

4 **el gato**
el gatoh

5 **el hámster**
el hamster

6 **el perro**
el perroh

1 Animals

Name the numbered animals
in Spanish.

bird **2**

hamster **5**

1 fish

4 cat

2 I like...

1 **Me gusta el fútbol.**
may goostah el footbol

2 **No me gusta el golf.**
noh may goostah el golf

3 **Me gusta pintar.**
may goostah peentar

4 **No me gustan las flores.**
noh may goostan las flores

2 I like...

Say the following in Spanish:

1 *I like soccer.*

2 *I don't like golf.*

3 *I like painting.*

4 *I don't like flowers.*

❸ *rabbit*

❻ *dog*

3 Hacer

Use the correct form of the verb **hacer** (*to do* or *to make*) in these sentences.

1 Vosotros _____ senderismo.

2 Ella _____ eso todos los días.

3 ¿Qué _____ tú?

4 Hoy no _____ frío.

5 ¿Qué _____ ellos esta noche?

6 Yo _____ natación.

3 Hacer

1 **hacéis**
ah<u>thays</u>

2 **hace**
<u>ah</u>thay

3 **haces**
<u>ah</u>thes

4 **hace**
<u>ah</u>thay

5 **hacen**
<u>ah</u>then

6 **hago**
<u>ah</u>goh

4 An invitation

You are invited for dinner. Join in the conversation, replying in Spanish following the English prompts.

¿Quieres venir a comer el viernes?
1 *I'm sorry, I'm busy.*

¿Qué tal el sábado?
2 *I'd love to.*

Ven con los niños.
3 *Thank you. What time?*

A las doce y media.
4 *That's good for me.*

4 An invitation

1 **Lo siento, estoy ocupado/-a.**
loh <u>syen</u>toh, e<u>stoy</u> okoo<u>pa</u>doh/-ah

2 **Encantado/-a.**
enkan<u>ta</u>doh/-ah

3 **Gracias. ¿A qué hora?**
<u>grath</u>yas. ah kay <u>orah</u>

4 **Me viene bien.**
may <u>byen</u>ay byen

Reinforce and progress

Regular practice is the key to maintaining and advancing your language skills. In this section you will find a variety of suggestions for reinforcing and extending your knowledge of Spanish. Many involve returning to exercises in the book and using the dictionaries to extend their scope. Go back through the lessons in a different order, mix and match activities to make up your own 15-minute daily program, or focus on topics that are of particular relevance to your current needs.

Keep warmed up
Revisit the Warm Up boxes to remind yourself of key words and phrases. Make sure you work your way through all of them on a regular basis.

1 Warm up

Say "I'm sorry"?
(pp.32–3)

What is the Spanish for "I'd like an appointment"?
(pp.22–3 and pp.32–3)

How do you say "when?" in Spanish?
(pp.32–3)

2 I'd like...

Say "I'd like" the following:

1 black coffee

churros **2**   sugar **3**

coffee with milk **4**

Review and repeat again
Work through a Review and Repeat lesson as a way of reinforcing words and phrases presented in the course. Return to the main lesson for any topic on which you are no longer confident.

Carry on conversing
Reread the In Conversation panels. Say both parts of the conversation, paying attention to the pronunciation. Where possible, try incorporating new words from the dictionary.

3 In conversation: taxi

A la Plaza de España, por favor.
ah lah plathah day espanyah, por fabor

Plaza de España, please.

Sí, de acuerdo, señor.
see, day akwairdo, senyor

Yes, certainly, sir.

¿Me puede dejar aq por favor?
may pweday dehar ahkee, por fabor

Can you drop me her please?

4 Useful phrases

Learn these phrases and then test yourself using the cover flap.

What time do you open/close?	**¿A qué hora abre/cierra?** ah kay orah ahbray/thyairrah
Where are the restrooms?	**¿Dónde están los servicios?** donday estan los serbeethyos
Is there access for wheelchairs?	**¿Hay acceso para sillas de ruedas?** ah-ee akthesoh parah seeyas day rwedas

Practice phrases
Return to the Useful Phrases and Put into Practice exercises. Test yourself using the cover flap. When you are confident, devise your own versions of the phrases, using new words from the dictionary.

Match, repeat, and extend
Remind yourself of words related to specific topics by returning to the Match and Repeat and Words to Remember exercises. Test yourself using the cover flap. Discover new words in that area by referring to the dictionary and menu guide.

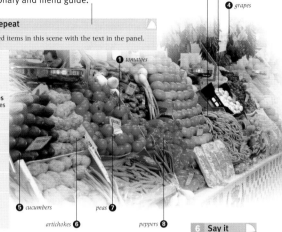

❷ *beans*

❸ *mushrooms*

❹ *grapes*

5   Match and repeat

Match the numbered items in this scene with the text in the panel.

1   **los tomates**
    los to<u>ma</u>tes

2   **las judías**
    las hoo<u>dee</u>as

3   **los champiñones**
    los champe<u>nyo</u>nes

4   **las uvas**
    las <u>oo</u>bas

5   **los pepinos**
    los pe<u>pee</u>nos

6   **las alcachofas**
    las alk<u>ach</u>ofas

7   **los guisantes**
    los ghee<u>san</u>tes

8   **los pimientos**
    los peem<u>yain</u>tos

❶ *tomatoes*

❺ *cucumbers*   *peas* ❼

artichokes ❻   *peppers* ❽

Say it again
The Say It exercises are a useful instant reminder for each lesson. Practice these, using your own vocabulary variations from the dictionary or elsewhere in the lesson.

6   Say it

The lawn needs <u>watering.</u>

Are there any trees?

The gardener comes on Fridays.

Using other resources

In addition to working with this book, try the following language extension ideas:

- Visit a Spanish-speaking country and try out your new skills with native speakers. Find out if there is a Spanish community near you. There may be shops, cafés, restaurants, and clubs. Try to visit some of these and use your Spanish to order food and drink and strike up conversations. Most native speakers will be happy to speak Spanish to you.

- Join a language class or club. There are usually evening and day classes available at a variety of different levels. Or you could start a club yourself if you have friends who are also interested in keeping up their Spanish.

- Look at Spanish magazines and newspapers. The pictures will help you to understand the text. Advertisements are also a useful way of expanding your vocabulary.

- Use the Internet, where you can find all kinds of websites for learning languages, some of which offer free online help and activities. You can also find Spanish websites for everything from renting a house to shampooing your pet. You can even access Spanish radio and TV stations online. Start by going to a Spanish search engine, such as *ozu.es*, and keying in a hobby or sport that interests you, or set yourself a challenge, such as finding a two-bedroom house for rent in Madrid.

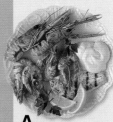

Menu guide

This guide lists the most common terms you may encounter on Spanish menus or when shopping for food. If you can't find an exact phrase, try looking up its component parts.

A

aceitunas *olives*
acelgas *spinach beet*
achicoria *chicory*
aguacate *avocado*
ahumados *smoked*
agua mineral *mineral water*
ajo *garlic*
al ajillo *with garlic*
a la parrilla *grilled*
a la plancha *grilled*
albaricoques *apricots*
albóndigas *meatballs*
alcachofas *artichokes*
alcaparras *capers*
al horno *baked*
allioli *garlic mayonnaise*
almejas *clams*
almejas a la marinera *clams stewed in wine and parsley*
almejas naturales *live clams*
almendras *almonds*
almíbar *syrup*
alubias *beans*
ancas de rana *frogs' legs*
anchoas *anchovies*
anguila *eel*
angulas *baby eels*
arenque *herring*
arroz a la cubana *rice with fried eggs and banana fritters*
arroz a la valenciana *rice with seafood*
arroz con leche *rice pudding*
asados *roast meat*
atún *tuna*
azúcar *sugar*

B

bacalao a la vizcaína *cod served with ham, peppers, and chili pepper*
bacalao al pil pil *cod served with chili pepper and garlic*
batido *milk shake*
bebidas *drinks*
berenjenas *eggplant*
besugo al horno *baked sea bream*
bistec de ternera *veal steak*
bonito *fish similar to tuna*

boquerones fritos *fried fresh anchovies*
brazo gitano *swiss roll*
brocheta de riñones *kidney kebabs*
buñuelos *fried pastries*
butifarra *Catalan sausage*

C

cabrito asado *roast kid*
cacahuetes *peanuts*
cachelada *pork stew with eggs, tomato, and onion*
café *coffee*
café con leche *coffee with steamed milk*
calabacines *zucchini*
calabaza *pumpkin*
calamares a la romana *squid rings in batter*
calamares en su tinta *squid cooked in their ink*
caldeirada *fish soup*
caldereta gallega *vegetable stew*
caldo de ... ... *soup*
caldo de gallina *chicken soup*
caldo de pescado *clear fish soup*
caldo gallego *vegetable soup*
caldo guanche *soup of potatoes, tomatoes, onions, and zucchini*
callos a la madrileña *tripe with chili pepper*
camarones *baby shrimp*
canela *cinnamon*
cangrejos *crabs*
caracoles *snails*
caramelos *sweets*
carnes *meats*
castañas *chestnuts*
cebolla *onion*
cebolletas *green onions*
centollo *spider crab*
cerdo *pork*
cerezas *cherries*
cerveza *beer*
cesta de frutas *selection of fresh fruit*
champiñones *mushrooms*
chanquetes *fish (similar to whitebait)*
chipirones *baby squid*
chipirones en su tinta *squid cooked in their ink*
chocos *cuttlefish*

chorizo *spicy sausage*
chuleta de buey *beef chop*
chuleta de cerdo *pork chop*
chuleta de cerdo empanada *breaded pork chop*
chuleta de cordero *lamb chop*
chuleta de cordero empanada *breaded lamb chop*
chuleta de ternera *veal chop*
chuleta de ternera empanada *breaded veal chop*
chuletas de lomo ahumado *smoked pork chops*
chuletitas de cordero *small lamb chops*
chuletón *large chop*
chuletón de buey *large beef chop*
churros *deep-fried pastry strips*
cigalas *crayfish*
cigalas cocidas *boiled crayfish*
ciruelas *plums*
ciruelas pasas *prunes*
cochinillo asado *roast suckling pig*
cocido *meat, chickpea, and vegetable stew*
cocktail de bogavante *lobster cocktail*
cocochas (de merluza) *hake stew*
cóctel de gambas *shrimp cocktail*
cóctel de langostinos *jumbo shrimp cocktail*
cóctel de mariscos *seafood cocktail*
codornices *quail*
codornices escabechadas *marinated quail*
codornices estofadas *braised quail*
col *cabbage*
coles de Bruselas *Brussels sprouts*
coliflor *cauliflower*
coñac *brandy*
conejo *rabbit*
conejo encebollado *rabbit with onions*
congrio *conger eel*

consomé con yema *consommé with egg yolk*
consomé de ave *fowl consommé*
contra de ternera con guisantes *veal stew with peas*
contrafilete de ternera *veal fillet*
copa *glass (of wine)*
copa de helado *ice cream, assorted flavors*
cordero asado *roast lamb*
cordero chilindrón *lamb stew with onion, tomato, peppers, and eggs*
costillas de cerdo *pork ribs*
crema catalana *crème brûlée*
cremada *dessert made with egg, sugar, and milk*
crema de... *cream of ... soup*
crema de legumbres *cream of vegetable soup*
crepe imperiale *crêpe suzette*
criadillas de tierra *truffles*
crocante *ice cream with chopped nuts*
croquetas *croquettes*
cuajada *curds*

D, E

dátiles *dates*
embutidos *sausages*
embutidos de la tierra *local sausages*
empanada gallega *fish pie*
empanada santiaguesa *fish pie*
empanadillas *small pies*
endivia *endive*
en escabeche *marinated*
ensalada *salad*
ensalada de arenque *fish salad*
ensalada ilustrada *mixed salad*
ensalada mixta *mixed salad*
ensalada simple *green salad*
ensaladilla rusa *Russian salad (potatoes, carrots, peas, and other vegetables in mayonnaise)*
entrecot a la parrilla *grilled entrecôte*
entremeses *hors d'oeuvres, appetizers*
escalope a la milanesa *breaded veal with cheese*
escalope a la parrilla *grilled veal*
escalope a la plancha *grilled veal*
escalope de lomo de cerdo *escalope of pork fillet*

escalope de ternera *veal escalope*
escalope empanado *breaded escalope*
escalopines al vino de Marsala *veal escalopes cooked in Marsala wine*
escalopines de ternera *veal escalopes*
espadín a la toledana *kebab*
espaguetis *spaghetti*
espárragos *asparagus*
espárragos trigueros *wild green asparagus*
espinacas *spinach*
espinazo de cerdo con patatas *stew of pork ribs with potatoes*
estofado *braised; stew*
estragón *tarragon*

F

fabada (asturiana) *bean stew with sausage*
faisán *pheasant*
faisán trufado *pheasant with truffles*
fiambres *cold meats*
fideos *thin pasta, noodles*
filete a la parrilla *grilled beef steak*
filete de cerdo *pork steak*
filete de ternera *veal steak*
flan *crème caramel*
frambuesas *raspberries*
fresas *strawberries*
fritos *fried*
fruta *fruit*

G

gallina en pepitoria *chicken stew with peppers*
gambas *shrimp*
gambas cocidas *boiled shrimp*
gambas en gabardina *shrimp in batter*
gambas rebozadas *shrimp in batter*
garbanzos *chickpeas*
garbanzos a la catalana *chickpeas with sausage, boiled eggs, and pine nuts*
gazpacho andaluz *cold tomato soup*
gelatina de ... ... *gelatin*
gratén de ... ... *au gratin (baked in a cream and cheese sauce)*
granizada *crushed ice drink*
gratinada/o *au gratin*
grelo *turnip*
grillado *grilled*
guisantes *peas*
guisantes salteados *sautéed peas*

H

habas *broad beans*
habichuelas *white beans*
helado *ice cream*
helado de vainilla *vanilla ice cream*
helado de turrón *nougat ice cream*
hígado *liver*
hígado de ternera *calves' liver*
hígado estofado *braised liver*
higos con miel y nueces *figs with honey and nuts*
higos secos *dried figs*
horchata (de chufas) *cold drink made from chufa nuts*
huevo hilado *egg yolk garnish*
huevos *eggs*
huevos a la flamenca *fried eggs with ham, tomato, and vegetables*
huevos cocidos *hard-boiled eggs*
huevos con patatas fritas *fried eggs and french fries*
huevos con picadillo *eggs with ground meat*
huevos duros *hard-boiled eggs*
huevos escalfados *poached eggs*
huevos pasados por agua *soft-boiled eggs*
huevos revueltos *scrambled eggs*

J

jamón *ham*
jamón con huevo hilado *ham with egg yolk garnish*
jamón serrano *cured ham*
jarra de vino *wine jug*
jerez *sherry*
jeta *pigs' cheeks*
judías verdes *green beans*
judías verdes a la española *bean stew*
judías verdes al natural *plain green beans*
jugo de ... ... *juice*

L

langosta *lobster*
langosta a la americana *lobster with brandy and garlic*
langosta a la catalana *lobster with mushrooms and ham in white sauce*
langosta fría con mayonesa *cold lobster with mayonnaise*

langostinos *jumbo shrimp*
langostinos dos salsas *jumbo shrimp cooked in two sauces*
laurel *bay leaves*
leche *milk*
leche frita *pudding made from milk and eggs*
leche merengada *cold milk with meringue*
lechuga *lettuce*
lengua de buey *ox tongue*
lengua de cordero *lambs' tongue*
lenguado a la romana *sole in batter*
lenguado meunière *sole meunière (floured sole fried in butter)*
lentejas *lentils*
lentejas aliñadas *lentils in vinaigrette dressing*
licores *liquor, liqueur*
liebre estofada *stewed hare*
lima *lime*
limón *lemon*
lombarda *red cabbage*
lomo curado *pork loin sausage*
lonchas de jamón *sliced, cured ham*
longaniza *cooked Spanish sausage*
lubina *sea bass*
lubina a la marinera *sea bass in a parsley sauce*

M

macedonia de fruta *fruit salad*
mahonesa *or* mayonesa *mayonnaise*
Málaga *a sweet wine*
mandarinas *tangerines*
manitas de cordero *lamb shank*
manos de cerdo *pigs' feet*
manos de cerdo a la parrilla *grilled pigs' feet*
mantecadas *small sponge cakes*
mantequilla *butter*
manzanas *apples*
mariscada *cold mixed shellfish*
mariscos del día *fresh shellfish*
mariscos del tiempo *seasonal shellfish*
medallones *steaks*
media de agua *half-bottle of mineral water*
mejillones *mussels*
mejillones a la marinera *mussels in a wine sauce*
melocotón *peach*
melón *melon*
menestra de legumbres *vegetable stew*

menú de la casa *set menu*
menú del día *set menu*
merluza *hake*
merluza a la cazuela *stewed hake*
merluza al ajo arriero *hake with garlic and chili pepper*
merluza a la riojana *hake with chili pepper*
merluza a la romana *hake steaks in batter*
merluza a la vasca *hake in a garlic sauce*
merluza en salsa *hake in sauce*
merluza en salsa verde *hake in a green (parsley and wine) sauce*
merluza fría *cold hake*
merluza frita *fried hake*
mermelada *jam*
mero *grouper (fish)*
mero en salsa verde *grouper in green (garlic and parsley) sauce*
mollejas de ternera fritas *fried sweetbreads*
morcilla *blood sausage*
morcilla de carnero *mutton blood sausage*
morros de cerdo *pigs' cheeks*
morros de vaca *cows' cheeks*
mortadela *salami-type sausage*
morteruelo *kind of pâté*

N, O

nabo *turnip*
naranjas *oranges*
nata *cream*
natillas *cold custard*
níscalos *wild mushrooms*
nueces *walnuts*
orejas de cerdo *pigs' ears*

P

paella *fried rice with seafood and/or meat*
paella castellana *meat paella*
paella valenciana *shellfish, rabbit, and chicken paella*
paleta de cordero lechal *shoulder of lamb*
pan *bread*
panache de verduras *vegetable stew*
panceta *bacon*
parrillada de caza *mixed grilled game*
parrillada de mariscos *mixed grilled shellfish*
pasas *raisins*
pastel de ternera *veal pie*
pasteles *cakes*

patatas a la pescadora *potatoes with fish*
patatas asadas *baked potatoes*
patatas bravas *potatoes in spicy tomato sauce*
patatas fritas *french fries*
patitos rellenos *stuffed duckling*
pato a la naranja *duck in orange sauce*
pavo *turkey*
pavo trufado *turkey stuffed with truffles*
pecho de ternera *breast of veal*
pechuga de pollo *breast of chicken*
pepinillos *pickles*
pepino *cucumber*
peras *pears*
percebes *edible barnacle*
perdices a la campesina *partridges with vegetables*
perdices a la manchega *partridges in red wine, garlic, herbs, and pepper*
perdices escabechadas *marinated partridges*
perejil *parsley*
perritos calientes *hot dogs*
pescaditos fritos *fried fish*
pestiños *sugared pastries flavored with aniseed*
pez espada *swordfish*
picadillo de ternera *ground veal*
pimienta *black pepper*
pimientos *peppers*
pimientos a la riojana *baked red peppers fried in oil and garlic*
pimientos morrones *a type of bell pepper*
pimientos verdes *green peppers*
piña al gratín *pineapple au gratin*
piña fresca *fresh pineapple*
pinchitos/pinchos *kebabs, snacks served in bars*
pinchos morunos *pork kebabs*
piñones *pine nuts*
pisto *ratatouille*
pisto manchego *vegetable marrow with onion and tomato*
plátanos *bananas*
plátanos flameados *flambéed bananas*
pollo *chicken*
pollo a la riojana *chicken with peppers and chili pepper*
pollo al ajillo *fried chicken with garlic*
pollo asado *roast chicken*
pollo braseado *braised chicken*
pollo en cacerola *chicken casserole*

pollo en pepitoria *chicken in wine with saffron, garlic, and almonds*

pollos tomateros con zanahorias *young chicken with carrots*

pomelo *grapefruit*

potaje castellano *thick broth*

potaje de ... ... *stew*

puchero canario *casserole of meat, chickpeas, and corn*

pulpitos con cebolla *baby octopus with onions*

pulpo *octopus*

puré de patatas *mashed potatoes, potato purée*

purrusalda *cod with leeks and potatoes*

Q

queso con membrillo *cheese with quince jelly*

queso de bola *Dutch cheese*

queso de Burgos *soft white cheese*

queso del país *local cheese*

queso de oveja *sheep's cheese*

queso gallego *a creamy cheese*

queso manchego *a hard, strong cheese*

quisquillas *shrimp*

R

rábanos *radishes*

ragout de ternera *veal ragoût*

rape a la americana *monkfish with brandy and herbs*

rape a la cazuela *stewed monkfish*

raya *skate*

rebozado *in batter*

redondo al horno *roast fillet of beef*

rellenos *stuffed*

remolacha *beet*

repollo *cabbage*

repostería de la casa *cakes baked on the premises*

requesón *cream cheese, cottage cheese*

revuelto de ... *scrambled eggs with ...*

revuelto de ajos tiernos *scrambled eggs with spring garlic*

revuelto de trigueros *scrambled eggs with asparagus*

revuelto mixto *scrambled eggs with mixed vegetables*

riñones *kidneys*

rodaballo *turbot (fish)*

romero *rosemary*

ron *rum*

roscas *sweet pastries*

S

sal *salt*

salchichas *sausages*

salchichas de Frankfurt *hot dog–type sausages*

salchichón *sausage similar to salami*

salmón ahumado *smoked salmon*

salmonetes *red mullet*

salmonetes en papillote *red mullet cooked in foil*

salmón frío *cold salmon*

salmorejo *sauce of bread, tomatoes, oil, vinegar, green pepper, and garlic*

salpicón de mariscos *shellfish in vinaigrette*

salsa *sauce*

salsa bechamel *white sauce*

salsa holandesa *hollandaise sauce*

sandía *watermelon*

sardinas a la brasa *barbecued sardines*

seco *dry*

semidulce *medium-sweet*

sesos *brains*

sesos a la romana *fried brains in batter*

sesos rebozados *brains in batter*

setas *mushrooms*

sidra *cider*

sobreasada *sausage with cayenne pepper*

solomillo *fillet steak*

solomillo con patatas *fillet steak with fries*

solomillo de ternera *fillet of veal*

solomillo de vaca *fillet of beef*

solomillo frío *cold roast beef*

sopa *soup*

sopa castellana *vegetable soup*

sopa de almendras *almond soup*

sopa de cola de buey *oxtail soup*

sopa de gallina *chicken soup*

sopa del día *soup of the day*

sopa de legumbres *vegetable soup*

sopa de marisco *fish and shellfish soup*

sopa de rabo de buey *oxtail soup*

sopa mallorquina *soup of tomato, meat, and eggs*

sopa sevillana *fish and mayonnaise soup*

soufflé de fresones *strawberry soufflé*

T

tallarines *noodles*

tallarines a la italiana *tagliatelle*

tarta *cake*

tarta de la casa *cake baked on the premises*

tarta de manzana *apple tart*

tencas *tench*

ternera asada *roast veal*

tocinillos del cielo *a very sweet crème caramel*

tomates *tomatoes*

tomillo *thyme*

torrijas *sweet pastries*

tortilla a la paisana *vegetable omelet*

tortilla a su gusto *omelet made to the customer's specifications*

tortilla de escabeche *fish omelet*

tortilla española *Spanish omelet with potato, onion, and garlic*

tortilla sacromonte *vegetable, brains, and sausage omelet*

tortillas variadas *assorted omelets*

tournedó *fillet steak*

trucha *trout*

trucha ahumada *smoked trout*

trucha escabechada *marinated trout*

truchas a la marinera *trout in wine sauce*

truchas molinera *trout meunière (floured trout fried in butter)*

trufas *truffles*

turrón *nougat*

U, V

uvas *grapes*

verduras *vegetables*

vieiras *scallops*

vino de mesa/blanco /rosado/tinto *table/ white/rosé/red wine*

Z

zanahorias a la crema *creamed carrots*

zarzuela de mariscos *seafood stew*

zarzuela de pescados y mariscos *fish and shellfish stew*

zumo de ... ... *juice*

Dictionary
English to Spanish

The gender of a Spanish noun is indicated by the word for *the*: **el** and **la** (masculine and feminine singular) or their plural forms **los** (masculine) and **las** (feminine). Spanish adjectives (adj) vary according to the gender and number of the word they describe, and the masculine form is shown here. In general, adjectives that end in **-o** adopt an **-a** ending in the feminine form, and those that end in **-e** usually stay the same. For the plural form, an **-s** is added.

A

a un/una
able: to be able poder
about: about sixteen alrededor de dieciséis
accelerator el acelerador
accident el accidente
accommodation el alojamiento
accountant el/la contable
ache el dolor
adapter el adaptador
address la dirección
adhesive el pegamento
admission charge el precio de entrada
after ... después de ...
aftershave el after-shave
again otra vez
against contra
agenda el orden del día
agency la agencia
AIDS el Sida
air el aire
air conditioning el aire acondicionado
aircraft el avión
airline la compañía aérea
air mail por avión
air mattress la colchoneta
airport el aeropuerto
airport bus el autobús del aeropuerto
aisle el pasillo
alarm clock el despertador
alcohol el alcohol
Algeria Argelia
all todo; *all the streets* todas las calles; *that's all* eso es todo
allergic alérgico
almost casi
alone solo
already ya
always siempre
am: I am soy/estoy

ambulance la ambulancia
America América
American el americano/la americana
and y; (after "i" or "h") e
ankle el tobillo
another otro
answering machine el contestador automático
antifreeze el anticongelante
antique shop el anticuario
antiseptic el antiséptico
apartment el apartamento, el piso
aperitif el aperitivo
appetite el apetito
apple la manzana
application form el impreso de solicitud
appointment (business) la cita; (at hairdresser) hora
apricot el albaricoque
April abril
are: you are (informal singular) eres/estás; (formal singular) es/está; (informal plural) sois/estáis; (formal plural) son/están; *we are* somos/estamos; *they are* son/están
arm el brazo
arrive llegar
art el arte
art gallery la galería de arte
artichoke la alcachofa
artist el/la artista
as: as soon as possible lo antes posible
ashtray el cenicero
asleep: he's asleep está dormido
aspirin la aspirina

asthmatic asmático
at: at the post office en Correos; *at night* por la noche; *at 3 o'clock* a las tres
athletic shoes los zapatos de deporte
Atlantic Ocean el Océano Atlántico
ATM el cajero automático
attic el ático
attractive (person) guapo; (object) bonito; (offer) atractivo
August agosto
aunt la tía
Australia Australia
Australian el australiano/la australiana; (adj) australiano
automatic automático
available disponible
away: is it far away? ¿está lejos?; *go away!* ¡váyase!
awful horrible
axe el hacha
axle el eje

B

baby el niño pequeño, el bebé
baby carriage el cochecito
baby wipes las toallitas para bebé
back (not front) la parte de atrás; (body) la espalda
backpack la mochila
bacon el bacon; *bacon and eggs* los huevos fritos con bacon
bad malo
bag la bolsa
bait el cebo
bake cocer al horno
bakery la pastelería
balcony el balcón

Balearic Islands las (Islas) Baleares

ball (soccer) el balon; (tennis, etc.) la pelota

ballpoint pen el bolígrafo

banana el plátano

band (musicians) la banda

bandage la venda; (adhesive) la tirita

bangs (hair) el flequillo

bank el banco

bank card la tarjeta de banco

banknote el billete de banco

bar (drinks) el bar

barbecue la barbacoa

barber la peluquería de caballeros

bargain la ganga

basement el sótano, la bodega

basin (sink) el lavabo

basket el cesto

basketball el baloncesto

bath el baño; *to have a bath* darse un baño

bathroom el cuarto de baño

battery (car) la batería; (flashlight, etc.) la pila

Bay of Biscay el Golfo de Vizcaya

be ser/estar

beach la playa

beach ball el balón de playa

beans las judías

beard la barba

beautiful (object) precioso; (person) guapo

beauty products los productos de belleza

because porque

bed la cama

bed linen la ropa de cama

bedroom el dormitorio

bedside lamp la lamparilla de noche

bedspread la colcha

beef la carne de vaca

beer la cerveza

before ... antes de ...

beginner el/la principiante

behind ... detrás de ...

beige beige

bell (church) la campana; (door) el timbre

below debajo de

belt el cinturón

beside al lado de

best (el) mejor

better mejor

between entre

bicycle la bicicleta

big grande

bill la cuenta

bird el pájaro

birthday el cumpleaños; *happy birthday!* ¡felicidades!

birthday present el regalo de cumpleaños

bite (by dog) la mordedura; (by insect) la picadura; (verb: by dog) morder; (by insect) picar

black negro

blackberries las moras

black currants las grosellas negras

blanket la manta

bleach la lejía; (verb: hair) teñir

blind (cannot see) ciego

blinds las persianas

blister la ampolla

blizzard la ventisca

blond(e) (adj) rubio

blood la sangre

blood test el análisis de sangre

blouse la blusa

blue azul

boarding pass la tarjeta de embarque

boat el barco; (small) la barca

body el cuerpo

boil (verb: water) hervir; (egg, etc.) cocer

boiled hervido

bolt (on door) el cerrojo; (verb) echar el cerrojo

bone el hueso

book el libro;(verb) reservar

bookstore la librería

boot (footwear) la bota

border el borde; (between countries) la frontera

boring aburrido

born: I was born in ... nací en ...

both: both of them los dos; *both of us* los dos; *both ... and ...* tanto ... como ...

bottle la botella

bottle opener el abrebotellas

bottom el fondo; (part of body) el trasero

bowl el cuenco

box la caja

box office la taquilla

boy el chico

boyfriend el novio

bra el sostén

bracelet la pulsera

brake el freno; (verb) frenar

branch (of company) la oficina

brandy el coñac

bread el pan

bread shop la panadería

breakdown (car) la avería; (nervous) la crisis nerviosa; *I've had a breakdown* (car) he tenido una avería

breakfast el desayuno

breathe respirar

bridge el puente; (game) el bridge

briefcase la cartera

British británico

brochure el folleto

broken roto

brooch el broche

brother el hermano

brown marrón; (hair) castaño; (skin) moreno

bruise el cardenal

brush (paint) la brocha; (cleaning) el cepillo; (hair) el cepillo del pelo; (verb: hair) cepillar el pelo

budget el presupuesto

bucket el cubo

building el edificio

bull el toro

bullfight la corrida de toros

bullfighter el torero

bullring la plaza de toros

bumper el parachoques

burglar el ladrón

burn la quemadura; (verb) quemar

bus el autobús

business el negocio; *it's none of your business* no es asunto suyo

business card la tarjeta de vista

bus station la estación de autobuses

busy (bar) concurrido; (phone) ocupado

but pero

butcher shop la carnicería

butter la mantequilla

button el botón

buy comprar

by: by the window junto a la ventana; *by Friday* para el viernes; *by myself* yo solo; *written by* escrito por

C

cabbage la col
cable car el teleférico
cable TV la television por cable
café el café
cage la jaula
cake (small) el pastel; (large) la tarta; *sponge cake* el bizcocho
calculator la calculadora
call: what's it called? ¿cómo se llama?
camcorder la videocámara
camera la máquina de fotos, la cámara de fotos
camper trailer la roulotte
camper van la autocaravana
campfire la hoguera
campground el camping
camshaft el árbol de levas
can (tin) la lata; (verb: to be able) poder; *can you ...?* ¿puede ...?; *I can't ... no puedo ...*
Canada Canadá
Canadian canadiense
canal el canal
Canaries las (Islas) Canarias
candle la vela
candy los caramelos (m)
can opener el abrelatas
cap (bottle) el tapón; (hat) la gorra
car el coche
car (train) el vagón
carburetor el carburador
card la tarjeta
cardigan sweater la rebeca
careful prudente; *be careful!* ¡cuidado!
caretaker el portero, el encargado
carpenter el carpintero
carpet la alfombra
carrot la zanahoria
carry-on luggage el equipaje de mano
car seat (for baby/child) el asiento infantil
cart el carrito
case (suitcase) la maleta
cash el dinero; cobrar (verb); *to pay cash* pagar al contado
cashier el cajero
cassette la cassette, la cinta

cassette player el cassette
castanets las castañuelas
Castile Castilla
Castilian castellano
castle el castillo
cat el gato
Catalonia Cataluña
catch (bus, etc.) coger
cathedral la catedral
Catholic (adj) católico
cauliflower la coliflor
cave la cueva
CD el disco compacto
ceiling el techo
cell phone el teléfono móvil, el teléfono celular
cemetery el cementerio
central heating la calefacción central
center el centro
certificate el certificado
chair la silla
change (money) el cambio; (verb: money) cambiar; (clothes) cambiarse; (trains, etc.) hacer transbordo
charger el cargador
check el cheque
checkbook el talonario de cheques
check-in (desk) la (el mostrador de) facturación
check in (verb) facturar
checkout (supermarket) la caja
cheers! (toast) ¡salud!
cheese el queso
cherry la cereza
chess el ajedrez
chest (part of body) el pecho; (furniture) el arcón
chest of drawers la cómoda
chewing gum el chicle
chicken el pollo
child el niño/la niña
children los niños
children's ward la sala de pediatría
chimney la chimenea
china la porcelana
chips las patatas fritas
chocolate el chocolate; *box of chocolates* la caja de bombones; *chocolate bar* la tableta de chocolate
chop (food) la chuleta; (verb: cut) cortar
Christmas la navidad
church la iglesia
cigar el puro
cigarette el cigarrillo
city la ciudad

class la clase
classical music la música clásica
clean (adj) limpio
cleaner la asistenta
clear (obvious) evidente; (water) claro
clever listo
client el cliente
clock el reloj
close (near) cerca
close (verb) cerrar
closed cerrado
clothes la ropa
clubs (cards) tréboles
coat el abrigo
coat hanger la percha
cockroach la cucaracha
cocktail party el coctel
coffee el café
coin la moneda
cold (illness) el resfriado; (adj) frío; *I have a cold* tengo un resfriado; *I'm cold* tengo frío
collar el cuello; (of animal) el collar
collection (stamps, etc.) la colección
color el color
color film la película en color
comb el peine; (verb) peinar
come venir; *I come from ... soy de ...; we came last week* llegamos la semana pasada; *come here!* ¡venga aquí!
come back volver
comforter el edredón
compartment el compartimento
complicated complicado
computer el ordenador
computer games los vídeo-juegos
concert el concierto
conditioner (hair) el acondicionador
condom el condón
conductor (bus) el cobrador; (orchestra) el director
conference la conferencia
conference room la sala de conferencias
congratulations! ¡enhorabuena!
consulate el consulado
contact lenses las lentes de contacto
contraceptive el anticonceptivo
contract el contrato
cook el cocinero/ la cocinera; (verb) guisar

cookie la galleta
cooking utensils los utensilios de cocina
cool fresco
cork el corcho
corkscrew el sacacorchos
corner (of street) la esquina; (of room) el rincón
corridor el pasillo
cosmetics los cosméticos
cost (verb) costar; *what does it cost?* ¿cuánto cuesta?
cotton el algodón
cotton balls el algodón
cough la tos; (verb) toser
cough drops las pastillas para la garganta
countertop el mostrador
country (state) el país
countryside el campo
cousin el primo/la prima
crab el cangrejo
cramp el calambre
crayfish las cigalas
crazy loco
cream (dairy) la nata; (lotion) la crema
credit card la tarjeta de crédito
crib el capazo
crowded lleno
cruise el crucero
crutches las muletas
cry (weep) llorar; (shout) gritar
cucumber el pepino
cuff links los gemelos
cup la taza
cupboard el armario
curlers los rulos
curls los rizos
curry el curry
curtain la cortina
cushion el cojín
customs la aduana
cut la cortadura; (verb) cortar
cycling el ciclismo

D

dad papá
dairy products los productos lácteos
damp húmedo
dance el baile; (verb) bailar
dangerous peligroso
dark oscuro; *dark blue* azul oscuro
daughter la hija
day el día
dead muerto
deaf sordo
dear (person) querido
December diciembre
deck of cards la baraja

decorator el pintor
deep profundo
delayed retrasado
deliberately a propósito
delicatessen la charcutería
delivery la entrega
dentist el/la dentista
dentures la dentadura postiza
deny negar
deodorant el desodorante
department el departamento
department store los grandes almacenes
departure la salida
departures las salidas
deposit la señal
designer el diseñador/la diseñadora
desk la mesa de escritorio
dessert el postre
develop (film) revelar
diabetic diabético
diamonds (jewels) los diamantes; (cards) los diamantes
diaper el pañal
diarrhea la diarrea
dictionary el diccionario
die morir
diesel (oil) fuel-oil; (adj: engine) diesel
different diferente; *that's different!* ¡eso es distinto!; *I'd like a different one* quisiera otro distinto
difficult difícil
dining room el comedor
dinner la cena
dinner party la cena
dirty sucio
disabled minusválido
discount el descuento
dish cloth el paño de cocina
dishwasher el lavavajillas
dishwashing liquid el lavavajillas
disposable diapers los pañales desechables
divorced divorciado
do hacer
dock el muelle
doctor el médico/la médica
document el documento
dog el perro
doll la muñeca
dollar el dólar
door la puerta
double room la habitación doble
doughnut el dónut
down hacia abajo

downtown el centro
dress el vestido
drink la bebida; (verb) beber; *would you like something to drink?* ¿quiere beber algo?
drinking water agua potable
drive (verb) conducir
driver el conductor
driver's license el carnet de conducir
drops las gotas
drunk borracho
dry seco; (sherry) fino
dry cleaner la tintorería
during durante
duster el trapo del polvo
duty-free libre de impuestos; *duty-free shop* el duty-free

E

each (every) cada; *20 euros each* veinte euros cada uno
ear (inner) el oído; (outer) la oreja; *ears* las orejas
early temprano
earrings los pendientes
east este; *the East* el Este
easy fácil
eat comer
egg el huevo
eggplant las berenjenas
eight ocho
eighteen dieciocho
eighty ochenta
either: either of them cualquiera de ellos; *either ... or ...* o bien ... o ...
elastic elástico
elbow el codo
electric eléctrico
electrician el/la electricista
electricity la electricidad
eleven once
else: something else algo más; *someone else* alguien más; *somewhere else* en otro sitio
email el email, el correo electrónico
email address la dirección de email
embarrassing embarazoso
embassy la embajada
embroidery el bordado
emergency la emergencia
emergency brake (train) el freno de emergencia
emergency department el servicio de urgencias

emergency exit la salida de emergencia

employee el empleado

empty vacío

end el final

engaged (marriage) prometido/prometida

engine (motor) el motor

engineering la ingeniería

England Inglaterra

English inglés

Englishman el inglés

Englishwoman la inglesa

enlargement la ampliación

enough bastante

entertainment las diversiones

entrance la entrada

envelope el sobre

epileptic epiléptico

eraser la goma de borrar

escalator la escalera mecánica

especially sobre todo

espresso el café solo

estimate el presupuesto

evening la tarde

every cada; *every day* todos los días

everyone todos

everything todo

everywhere por todas partes

example el ejemplo; *for example* por ejemplo

excellent excelente

excess baggage exceso de equipaje

exchange (verb) cambiar

exchange rate el cambio

excursion la excursión

excuse me! (to get attention) ¡oiga, por favor!; (when sneezing, etc.) ¡perdón!; *excuse me, please* (to get past) ¿me hace el favor?

executive el ejecutivo

exhaust el tubo de escape

exhibition la exposición

exit la salida

expensive caro

expressway la autopista

extension cord el cable alargador

eye el ojo

eyebrow la ceja

F

face la cara

faint (unclear) tenue; (verb) desmayarse; *I feel faint* estoy mareado

fair la feria; *it's not fair* no hay derecho

false teeth la dentadura postiza

family la familia

fan (enthusiast) el fan; (soccer) el hincha; (ventilator) el ventilador; (handheld) el abanico

fantastic fantástico

far lejos; *how far is it to ...?* ¿qué distancia hay a ...?

fare el billete, la tarifa

farm la granja

farmer el granjero

fashion la moda

fast rápido

fat (adj) gordo; (on meat) la grasa

father el padre

faucet el grifo

fax el fax; enviar por fax (verb)

February febrero

feel (touch) tocar; *I feel hot* tengo calor; *I feel like ...* me apetece ...; *I don't feel well* no me encuentro bien

felt-tip pen el rotulador

fence la cerca

ferry el ferry

fiancé el prometido

fiancée la prometida

field (of grass, etc.) el campo; (of study) la especialidad

fifteen quince

fifty cincuenta

fig el higo

figures los números

filling (in tooth) el empaste; (in sandwich, cake) el relleno

film la película

filter el filtro

filter papers los papeles de filtro

finger el dedo

fire el fuego; (blaze) el incendio

fire extinguisher el extintor

fireplace la chimenea

fireworks los fuegos artificiales

first primero; *first aid* primeros auxilios

first class de primera

first floor el primer piso

first name el nombre de pila

fish el pez; (food) el pescado

fishing la pesca; *to go fishing* ir a pescar

fishmonger la pescadería

five cinco

flag la bandera

flash (camera) el flash

flashlight la linterna

flat (level) plano

flat tire la rueda pinchada

flavor el sabor

flea la pulga

flea spray el spray antipulgas

flight el vuelo

floor el suelo; (story) el piso

flour la harina

flower la flor

flowerbed el parterre

flute la flauta

fly (insect) la mosca; (verb: of plane, insect) volar; (of person) viajar en avión

fog la niebla

folk music la música folklórica

food la comida

food poisoning la intoxicación alimenticia

foot el pie

for: for me para mí; *what for?* ¿para qué?; *for a week* (para) una semana

foreigner el extranjero/ la extranjera

forest el bosque; (tropical) la selva

forget olvidar

fork el tenedor; (garden) la horca

forty cuarenta

fountain la fuente

fountain pen la (pluma) estilográfica

four cuatro

fourteen catorce

fourth cuarto

France Francia

free (not engaged) libre; (no charge) gratis

freezer el congelador

French francés

french fries las patatas fritas

Friday viernes

fried frito

friend el amigo/la amiga

friendly simpático

front: in front of ... delante de ...

frost la escarcha

frozen foods los congelados

fruit la fruta

fruit juice el zumo de frutas
fry freír
frying pan la sartén
full lleno; *I'm full* estoy lleno
full board pensión completa
funny divertido; (odd) raro
furniture los muebles

G

garage (for parking) el garage; (for repairs) el taller
garbage la basura
garbage bag la bolsa de basura
garden el jardín
garden center el vivero
garlic el ajo
gasoline la gasolina
gas-permeable lenses las lentes de contacto semi-rígidas
gas station la gasolinera
gate la puerta, la verja; (at airport) la puerta de embarque
gay (homosexual) gay
gearbox la caja de cambios
gear stick la palanca de velocidades
gel (hair) el gel
German alemán
Germany Alemania
get (fetch) traer; *have you got ...?* ¿tiene ...?; *to get the train* coger el tren
get back: we get back tomorrow nos volvemos mañana; *to get something back* recobrar algo
get in (of train, etc.) subirse; (of person) llegar
get off (bus, etc.) bajarse
get on (bus, etc.) subirse
get out bajarse; (bring out) sacar
get up (rise) levantarse
Gibraltar Gibraltar
gift el regalo
gin la ginebra
ginger (spice) el jengibre
girl la chica
girlfriend la novia
give dar
glad alegre
glass (material) el cristal; (for drinking) el vaso, la copa

glasses las gafas
gloss prints las copias con brillo
gloves los guantes
glue el pegamento
go ir
gold el oro
good bueno; *good!* ¡bien!
good afternoon buenas tardes
goodbye adiós
good evening buenas noches
good morning buenos días
government el gobierno
granddaughter la nieta
grandfather el abuelo
grandmother la abuela
grandparents los abuelos
grandson el nieto
grapes las uvas
grass la hierba
gray gris
Great Britain Gran Bretaña
green verde
greengrocer la verdulería
grill la parrilla
grilled a la plancha
grocery store el ultramarinos, la tienda de comestibles
ground floor la planta baja
groundsheet la lona impermeable, el suelo aislante
guarantee la garantía; (verb) garantizar
guest la invitada
guide el/la guía
guide book la guía turística
guided tour la visita con guía
guitar la guitarra
gun (rifle) la escopeta; (pistol) la pistola
gym el centro deportivo

H

hair el pelo
haircut el corte de pelo
hairdryer el secador (de pelo)
hair salon la peluquería
hairspray la laca
half medio; *half an hour* media hora
half board media pensión
ham el jamón
hamburger la hamburguesa
hammer el martillo
hamster el hámster

hand la mano
handbag el bolso
handbrake el freno de mano
handle (door) el picaporte
handshake el apretón de manos
handsome guapo
handyman el albañil
hangover la resaca
happy contento, feliz
harbor el puerto
hard duro; (difficult) difícil
hardware store la ferretería
hat el sombrero; (woollen) el gorro
have tener; *I don't have ...* no tengo ...; *do you have ...?* ¿tiene ...?; *I have to go* tengo que irme ; *can I have ...?* ¿me pone ...?
hay fever la fiebre del heno
he él
head la cabeza
headache el dolor de cabeza
headlights los faros
headphones los auriculares
hear oír
hearing aid el audífono
heart el corazón
hearts (cards) los corazones
heater la estufa
heating la calefacción
heavy pesado
hedge el seto
heel el talón; (shoe) el tacón
hello hola; (on phone) dígame
help la ayuda; (verb) ayudar
hepatitis la hepatitis
her: it's for her es para ella; *her book* su libro; *her shoes* sus zapatos; *it's hers* es suyo; *give it to her* déselo
high alto
highway code el código de la circulación
hiking el senderismo
hill el monte
him: it's for him es para él; *give it to him* déselo
his: his book su libro; *his shoes* sus zapatos; *it's his* es suyo
history la historia
hitchhike hacer auto-stop
HIV positive seropositivo
hobby el hobby

home la casa; *at home* en casa
homeopathy la homeopatía
honest honrado; (sincere) sincero
honey la miel
honeymoon el viaje de novios
horn (car) el claxon; (animal) el cuerno
hood (car) el capó
horrible horrible
hospital el hospital
hostess la anfitriona
hour la hora
house la casa
household products los productos del hogar
hovercraft el aerodeslizador
how? ¿cómo?
how are you? ¿qué tal?
hundred cien
hungry: I'm hungry tengo hambre
hurry: I'm in a hurry tengo prisa
husband el marido
hydrofoil la hidroaleta

I

I yo
ice el hielo
ice cream el helado
ice skates los patines para hielo
if si
ignition el encendido
immediately inmediatamente
impossible imposible
in en; *in English* en inglés; *in the hotel* en el hotel; *in Barcelona* en Barcelona; *he's not in* no está
included incluido
indigestion indigestión
inexpensive barato
infection la infección
information la información
inhaler (for asthma, etc.) el spray, el inhalador
injection la inyección
injury la herida
ink la tinta
inn la fonda
inner tube la cámara (neumática)
insect el insecto
insect repellent la loción anti-mosquitos
insomnia el insomnio
instant coffee el café instantáneo
insurance el seguro
interesting interesante

Internet el internet
interpret interpretar
interpreter el/la intérprete
invitation la invitación
invoice la factura
Ireland Irlanda
Irish irlandés/ irlandesa
iron (metal) el hierro; (for clothes) la plancha; (verb) planchar
is es/está
island la isla
it lo/la
Italian (adj) italiano/ italiana (m/f)
Italy Italia
its su

J

jacket la chaqueta
jam la mermelada
January enero
jazz el jazz
jeans los tejanos, los vaqueros
jellyfish la medusa
jeweler la joyería
job el trabajo
jog (verb) hacer footing
jogging suit el chandal
joke la broma; (funny story) el chiste
journey el viaje
juice el zumo
July julio
June junio
just (only) sólo; *it's just arrived* acaba de llegar

K

kerosene la parafina
key la llave
keyboard el teclado
kidney el riñón
kilo el kilo
kilometer el kilómetro
kitchen la cocina
knee la rodilla
knife el cuchillo
knit hacer punto
knitwear los artículos de punto
know saber; (person, place) conocer; *I don't know* no sé

L

label la etiqueta
lace el encaje
laces (shoe) los cordones (de los zapatos)
lady la señora
lake el lago
lamb el cordero
lamp la lámpara, el flexo

lampshade la pantalla
land la tierra; (verb) aterrizar
language el idioma
large grande
last (final) último; *at last!* ¡por fin!; *last week* la semana pasada
late: it's getting late se está haciendo tarde; *the bus is late* el autobús se ha retrasado
later más tarde
laugh reír
laundromat la lavandería automática
laundry (dirty) la ropa sucia; (washed) la colada
laundry detergent el jabón de lavadora, el detergente
law el derecho
lawn el césped
lawn mower la maquina cortacésped
lawyer el abogado/ la abogada
laxative el laxante
lazy perezoso
leaf la hoja
leaflet el folleto
learn aprender
leash la correa
leather el cuero
lecture hall el anfiteatro
left (not right) izquierdo; *there's nothing left* no queda nada
leg la pierna
lemon el limón
lemonade la limonada
length la longitud
lens la lente
less menos
lesson la clase
letter (mail) la carta; (of alphabet) la letra
lettuce la lechuga
library la biblioteca
license el permiso
license plate la matrícula
life la vida
lift el ascensor
light la luz; (weight) ligero; (not dark) claro
light bulb la bombilla
lighter el encendedor
lighter fuel el gas para el encendedor
light meter el fotómetro
like: I like ... me gusta ...; *I like swimming* me gusta nadar; *it's like ...* es como ...; *like this one* como éste
lime (fruit) la lima

line la cola; (phone, etc.) línea; (verb) hacer cola
lipstick la barra de labios
liqueur el licor
list la lista
liter el litro
literature la literatura
litter la basura
little (small) pequeño; *it's a little big* es un poco grande; *just a little* sólo un poquito
liver el hígado
living room el cuarto de estar
lobster la langosta
lollipop el chupa-chups
long largo
lost property office la oficina de objetos perdidos
lot: a lot mucho
loud alto
lounge (in house) el cuarto de estar; (in hotel, etc.) el salón
love el amor; (verb) querer; *I love Spain* me encanta España
lover el/la amante
low bajo
luck: good luck! ¡suerte!
luggage el equipaje
luggage rack la rejilla de equipajes
lunch la comida

M

madam señora
magazine la revista
mail el correo; (verb) echar al correo
mailbox el buzón
mail carrier el cartero
main course el plato principal
main road la calle principal
Majorca Mallorca
make hacer
make-up el maquillaje
man el hombre
manager el/la gerente, el jefe; (hotel) el director/la directora
many muchos/muchas; *many thanks* muchas gracias; *many people* mucha gente; *how many* ¿cuántos?; *too many* demasiados; *not many* no muchos
map el mapa; *town map/plan* el plano
marble el mármol
March marzo
margarine la margarina

market el mercado
marmalade la mermelada de naranja
married casado
mascara el rímel
mass (church) la misa
match (light) la cerilla; (sports) el partido
material (cloth) la tela
matter: it doesn't matter no importa
mattress el colchón
May mayo
maybe quizás
me: it's for me es para mí; *give it to me* démelo
meal la comida
mean: what does this mean? ¿qué significa esto?
meat la carne
mechanic el mecánico
medicine la medicina
Mediterranean el Mediterráneo
medium (sherry) amontillado
medium-dry (wine) semi-seco
meeting la reunión
melon el melón
menu la carta; *set menu* el menú (del día)
message el recado, el mensaje
metro station le estación de metro
microwave el microondas
middle: in the middle en el centro
midnight medianoche
milk la leche
mine: it's mine es mío
mineral water el agua mineral
minute el minuto
mirror el espejo
Miss Señorita
mistake la equivocación
modem el modem
Monday lunes
money el dinero
monitor el monitor
month el mes
monument el monumento
moon la luna
moped el ciclomotor
more más
morning la mañana; *in the morning* por la mañana
Morocco Marruecos
mosaic el mosaico
mosquito el mosquito
mother la madre
motorboat la motora
motorcycle la motocicleta
mountain la montaña

mountain bike la bicicleta de montaña
mouse el ratón
mousse (for hair) la espuma moldeadora
mouth la boca
move (verb: something) mover; (oneself) moverse; (house) mudarse de casa; *don't move!* ¡no se mueva!
movie la película
movie theater el cine
Mr. Señor
Mrs. Señora
much: much better mucho mejor; *much slower* mucho más despacio
mug la jarrita
Mum mama
museum el museo
mushrooms los champiñones, las setas
music la música
musical instrument el instrumento musical
musician el músico
music system el equipo de música
mussels los mejillones
must (to have to) tener que *I must ...* tengo que ...
mustache el bigote
mustard la mostaza
my: my book mi libro; *my keys* mis llaves

N

nail (metal) el clavo; (finger) la uña
nail clippers el cortauñas
nailfile la lima de uñas
nail polish el esmalte de uñas
name el nombre; *what's your name?* ¿cómo se llama usted?; *my name is...* me llamo...
napkin la servilleta
narrow estrecho
near: near the door junto a la puerta; *near New York* cerca de New York
necessary necesario
neck el cuello
necklace el collar
need (verb) necesitar; *I need ...* necesito ...; *there's no need* no hace falta
needle la aguja
negative (photo) el negativo

neither: neither of them ninguno de ellos; *neither ... nor ...* ni ... ni ...

nephew el sobrino

never nunca

new nuevo

news las noticias

newspaper el periódico

newsstand el kiosko de periódicos

New Zealand Nueva Zelanda

New Zealander el neozelandés/ la neozelandesa

next próximo, siguiente; *next week* la semana que viene; *what next?* ¿y ahora qué?

nice bonito; (pleasant) agradable; (to eat) bueno

niece la sobrina

night la noche

nightclub la discoteca

nightgown el camisón

night porter el vigilante nocturno

nightstand la mesilla de noche

nine nueve

nineteen diecinueve

ninety noventa

no (response) no; *I have no money* no tengo dinero

nobody nadie

noisy ruidoso

noon mediodía

north el norte

Northern Ireland Irlanda del Norte

nose la nariz

not no; *he's not ...* no es/está ...

notebook el cuaderno

notepad el bloc

nothing nada

novel la novela

November noviembre

now ahora

nowhere en ninguna parte

nudist el/la nudista

number el número

nurse el enfermo/ la enfermera

nut (fruit) la nuez; (for bolt) la tuerca

O

oars los remos

occasionally de vez en cuando

occupied ocupado

October octubre

octopus el pulpo

of de

office (place) la oficina; (room) el despacho

office block el bloque de oficinas

often a menudo

oil el aceite

ointment la pomada

OK vale

old viejo; *how old are you?* ¿cuántos años tiene?

olive la aceituna

olive oil el aceite de oliva

olive tree el olivo

omelet la tortilla

on ... en ...

one uno

onion la cebolla

only sólo

open (adj) abierto; (verb) abrir

opening times el horario de apertura

operating room el quirófano

operation la operación

operator la operadora

across from: across from the hotel enfrente del hotel

optician el/la oculista

or o

orange (fruit) la naranja; (color) naranja

orchestra la orquesta

order el pedido

organ (music) el órgano

other: the other (one) el otro

our nuestro; *it's ours* es nuestro

out: he's out no está

outside fuera; *external* externa

oven el horno

over ... encima de ...; (more than) más de ...; *it's over the road* está al otro lado de la calle; *when the party is over* cuando termine la fiesta; *over there* allí

overpass el paso elevado

oyster la ostra

P

package el paquete

packet el paquete; (cigarettes) la cajetilla; (candy, chips) la bolsa

padlock el candado

page la página

pain el dolor

paint la pintura

pair el par

pajamas el pijama

palace el palacio

pale pálido

pancakes las crepes

pants el pantalón

pantyhose las medias, los pantis

paper el papel; (newspaper) el periódico

pardon? ¿cómo dice?

parents los padres

park el parque; (verb) aparcar; *no parking* prohibido aparcar

parking lot el aparcamiento

parsley el perejil

part (hair) la raya

party (celebration) la fiesta; (group) el grupo; (political) el partido

passenger el pasajero

pass (in car) adelantar

passport el pasaporte

password la contraseña

pasta la pasta

path el camino

pavement la acera

pay pagar

payment el pago

peach el melocotón

peanuts los cacahuetes

pear la pera

pearl la perla

peas los guisantes

pedestrian el peatón

pedestrian zone la zona peatonal

peg la pinza

pen la pluma

pencil el lápiz

pencil sharpener el sacapuntas

penknife la navaja

pen pal el amigo/ la amiga por correspondencia

people la gente

pepper la pimienta; (red, green) el pimiento

peppermints las pastillas de menta

per: per night por noche

perfect perfecto

perfume el perfume

perhaps quizás

perm la permanente

pet passport el pasaporte de animales

pets los animales de compañía; los animales domésticos

pharmacy la farmacia

phone book la guía telefónica

phone booth la cabina telefónica

phone card la tarjeta telefónica

photocopier la fotocopiadora

photograph la foto(grafía); (verb) fotografiar

photographer el fotógrafo

phrase book el libro de frases

piano el piano

pickpocket el carterista

pickup (postal) la recogida

picnic el picnic

piece el pedazo

pill la pastilla

pillow la almohada

pilot el piloto

PIN el pin

pin el alfiler

pine (tree) el pino

pineapple la piña

pink rosa

pipe (for smoking) la pipa; (for water) la tubería

piston el piston

pizza la pizza

place el lugar; *at your place* en su casa

planner la agenda

plant la planta

plastic el plástico

plastic bag la bolsa de plástico

plastic wrap el plástico para envolver

plate el plato

platform (train) el andén

play (theater) la obra de teatro; (verb) jugar

please por favor

pleased to meet you encantado/encantada

plug (electrical) el enchufe; (sink) el tapón

plumber el fontanero/la fontanera

pocket el bolsillo

poison el veneno

police la policía

police officer el policía

police report la denuncia

police station la comisaría

politics la política

poor pobre; (bad quality) malo

pop music la música pop

pork la carne de cerdo

port (harbor) el puerto; (drink) el oporto

porter (hotel) el conserje

Portugal Portugal

Portuguese portugués

possible posible

postcard la postal

poster el póster

post office (la oficina de) Correos

potato la patata

poultry las aves

pound (sterling) la libra

powder el polvo; (cosmetic) los polvos

prefer preferir

pregnant embarazada

prescription la receta

pretty bonito; (quite) bastante

price el precio

priest el cura

printer la impresora

private privado

problem el problema

profession la profesión

professor el catedrático; *professor* (university) el profesor/la profesora de universidad

profits los beneficios

prohibited prohibido

protection factor (SPF) el factor de protección

public público

public holiday el día de fiesta

public swimming pool la piscina municipal

pull tirar de

puncture el pinchazo

purple morado

purse la cartera, el monedero

push empujar

put poner

Pyrenees los Pirineos

Q

quality la calidad

quarter el cuarto

question la pregunta

quick rápido

quiet tranquilo; (person) callado

quite (fairly) bastante; (fully) completamente

R

rabbit el conejo

radiator el radiador

radio la radio

radish el rábano

rake el rastrillo

railroad el ferrocarril

rain la lluvia

raincoat la gabardina

rainforest la selva

raisins las pasas

raspberry la frambuesa

rare (uncommon) raro; (steak) poco hecho, poco pasado

rat la rata

razor blades las cuchillas de afeitar

read leer

ready listo

receipt el recibo

reception la recepción

receptionist el/la recepcionista

record (music) el disco; (sports, etc.) el récord

record player el tocadiscos

record store la tienda de discos

red rojo; (wine) tinto

refreshments los refrescos

refrigerator el frigorífico

registered mail correo certificado

relative el pariente

relax relajarse; (rest) descansar

religion la religión

remember; I remember me acuerdo; *I don't remember* no me acuerdo

rent (verb) alquilar

repair arreglar

report el informe

reservation la reserva

rest (remainder) el resto; (verb: relax) descansar

restaurant el restaurante

restaurant car el vagón-restaurante

restrooms los servicios

return (come back) volver; (give back) devolver

rice el arroz

rich rico

right (correct) correcto; (not left) derecho

ring (for finger) el anillo

ripe maduro

river el río

road la carretera

roasted asado

robbery el robo

rock (stone) la roca

roll (bread) el bollo

roof el tejado

room la habitación; (space) el sitio

room service el servicio de habitaciones

rope la cuerda

rose la rosa

round (circular) redondo

roundabout la rotonda

round-trip ticket el billete de ida y vuelta

row (verb) remar

rowing boat la barca de remos

rubber (material) la goma

rubber band la goma

ruby (stone) el rubí

rug (mat) la alfombra; (blanket) la manta

rugby el rugby

ruins las ruinas

ruler (for measuring) la regla

rum el ron

run (verb) correr

runway la pista

S

sad triste

safe (not dangerous) seguro

safety pin el imperdible

sailboard la tabla de windsurfing

sailing la vela

salad la ensalada

sale (at reduced prices) las rebajas

sales las ventas

salmon el salmón

salt la sal

same: the same dress el mismo vestido; *the same people* la misma gente; *same again, please* lo mismo otra vez, por favor

sand la arena

sandals las sandalias

sand dunes las dunas

sandwich el bocadillo

sanitary napkins las compresas

Saturday sábado

sauce la salsa

saucepan el cazo

saucer el platillo

sauna la sauna

sausage la salchicha

say decir; *what did you say?* ¿qué ha dicho?; *how do you say ...?* ¿cómo se dice ...?

scarf la bufanda; (head) el pañuelo

schedule el programa, el horario

school la escuela

science las ciencias

scissors las tijeras

Scotland Escocia

Scottish escocés/escocesa

screen la pantalla

screw el tornillo

screwdriver el destornillador

sea el mar

seafood los mariscos

seat el asiento

seat belt el cinturón de seguridad

second el segundo

second class de segunda

see ver; *I can't see* no veo; *I see* comprendo

self-employed (person) el autónomo/ la autónoma

sell vender

seminar el seminario

send mandar

separate (adj) distinto

separated separado

September septiembre

serious serio

seven siete

seventeen diecisiete

seventy setenta

several varios

sew coser

shampoo el champú

shave el afeitado; *to shave* afeitarse

shaving foam la espuma de afeitar

shawl el chal

she ella

sheet la sábana; (of paper) la hoja

shell la concha

shellfish mariscos

sherry el jerez

ship el barco

shirt la camisa

shoelaces los cordones de los zapatos

shoe polish la crema de zapatos

shoes los zapatos

shoe store la zapatería

shopping la compra; *to go shopping* ir de compras

short corto; (height) bajo

shorts los pantalones cortos

shoulder el hombro

shower (bath) la ducha; (rain) el chaparrón

shower gel el gel de ducha

shrimp las quisquillas, las gambas

shutter (camera) el obturador; (window) el postigo

sick: I feel sick tengo náuseas; *to be sick* (vomit) devolver

side (edge) el borde

side lights las luces de posición

sights: the sights of ... los lugares de interés de ...

sightseeing el turismo

silk la seda

silver (metal) la plata; (color) plateado

simple sencillo

sing cantar

single (ticket) de ida; (only) único; (unmarried) soltero/soltera

single room la habitación individual

sink el fregadero

sister la hermana

six seis

sixteen dieciséis

sixty sesenta

skid patinar

skiing: to go skiing ir a esquiar

skin cleanser la leche limpiadora

ski resort la estación de esquí

skirt la falda

skis los esquís

sky el cielo

sleep el sueño; (verb) dormir

sleeper car el coche-cama

sleeping bag el saco de dormir

sleeping pill el somnífero

sleeve la manga

slip (underwear) la combinación

slippers las zapatillas

slow lento

small pequeño

smell el olor; (verb) oler

smile la sonrisa; (verb) sonreír

smoke el humo; (verb) fumar

snack la comida ligera

snow la nieve

so: so good tan bueno; *not so much* no tanto

soaking solution (for contact lenses) la solución limpiadora

soap el jabón

soccer el fútbol; (ball) el balón

socks los calcetines

soda water la soda

sofa el sofa

soft blando

soil la tierra

somebody alguien

somehow de algún modo

something algo

sometimes a veces

somewhere en alguna parte

son el hijo

song la canción

sorry! ¡perdón!; *I'm sorry* perdón/lo siento; *sorry?* (pardon) ¿cómo dice?

soup la sopa

south el sur

South America Sudamérica

souvenir el recuerdo

spade la pala

spades (cards) las picas

Spain España

Spaniard el español/la española

sparkling water el agua con gas

speak hablar; *do you speak ...?* ¿habla ...?; *I don't speak ...* no hablo ...

speed la velocidad

speed limit el límite de velocidad

spider la araña

spinach las espinacas

spoon la cuchara

sports el deporte

spring (mechanical) el muelle; (season) la primavera

square (in town) la plaza; (adj) cuadrado

staircase la escalera

stairs las escaleras

stamp el sello

stapler la grapadora

star la estrella

start (beginning) el principio; (verb) empezar

starters los entrantes

statement la declaración

station la estación

statue la estatua

steak el filete

steal robar; *it's been stolen* lo han robado

steamed al vapor

steamer (boat) el vapor

stepdaughter la hijastra

stepfather el padrastro

stepmother la madrastra

stepson el hijastro

still water el agua sin gas

stockings las medias

stomach el estómago

stomach-ache el dolor de estómago

stop (bus) la parada; (verb) parar; *stop!* ¡alto!

store la tienda

storm la tormenta

stove la cocina

stove fuel el camping-gas

strawberries las fresas

stream (small river) el arroyo

street la calle

string la cuerda

stroller la sillita de ruedas

strong fuerte

student el/la estudiante

stuffy sofocante

stupid estúpido

suburbs las afueras

subway el metro

sugar el azúcar

suit (clothing) el traje; *it suits you* te sienta bien

suitcase la maleta

sun el sol

sunbathe tomar el sol

sunburn la quemadura de sol

Sunday domingo

sunglasses las gafas de sol

sunny: it's sunny hace sol

sunshade la sombrilla

sunstroke la insolación

suntan: to get a suntan broncearse

suntan lotion la loción bronceadora

suntanned bronceado

supermarket el supermercado

supper la cena

supplement el suplemento

suppository el supositorio

sure seguro

surname el apellido

suspenders (clothing) los tirantes

sweat el sudor; (verb) sudar

sweater el jersey

sweatshirt la sudadera

sweet (adj: not sour) dulce

swim (verb) nadar

swimming la natación

swimming pool la piscina

swimming trunks el bañador

swimsuit el bañador, el traje de baño

switch el interruptor

synagogue la sinagoga

syringe la jeringuilla

syrup el jarabe

T

table la mesa

tablet la pastilla

take tomar

take off el despegue

talcum powder los polvos de talco

talk la charla; (verb) hablar

tall alto

tampons los tampones

tangerine la mandarina

tapestry el tapiz

taxi el taxi

taxi stand la parada de taxis

tea el té

teakettle el hervidor de agua

teacher el profesor/la profesora

technician el técnico

telephone el teléfono; (verb) llamar por teléfono

television la televisión

temperature la temperatura; (fever) la fiebre

ten diez

tennis el tenis

tent la tienda

tent peg la estaquilla, la estaca

tent pole el mástil

terminal la terminal

terrace la terraza

test la prueba

than que

thank (verb) agradecer; *thank you* gracias; *thanks* gracias

that ese/esa, eso; *that bus* ese autobús; *that man* ese hombre; *that woman* esa mujer; *what's that?* ¿qué es eso?; *I think that ...* creo que ...; *that one* ése/ésa

the el/la; (plural) los/las

theater el teatro

their: their room su habitación; *their books* sus libros; *it's theirs* es suyo

them: it's for them es para ellos/ellas; *give it to them* déselo

then entonces; (after) después

there allí; *there is/are ...* hay ...; *is/are there ...?* ¿hay ...?

these: these men estos hombres; *these women* estas mujeres; *these are mine* éstos son míos

they ellos/ellas

thick grueso

thief el ladrón

thin delgado

think pensar; *I think so* creo que sí; *I'll think about it* lo pensaré

third tercero

thirsty: I'm thirsty tengo sed

thirteen trece

thirty treinta

this: this one éste/ésta; *this man* este hombre; *this woman* esta mujer; *what's this?* ¿qué es esto?; *this is Mr. ...* éste es el señor ...

those: those men esos
   hombres; *those
   women* esas mujeres
thousand mil
throat la garganta
through por
three tres
thumbtack la chincheta
thunderstorm
   la tormenta
Thursday jueves
ticket (train, etc.)
   el billete; (theater,
   etc.) la entrada
ticket office la taquilla
tide la marea
tie la corbata; (verb)
   atar
tight ajustado
time tiempo; *what's the
   time?* ¿qué hora es?
tin la hojalata
tip (end) la punta;
   (money) la propina
tire el neumático
tired cansado
tire iron la llave de las
   tuercas
tissues los pañuelos de
   papel
to: to America a
   América; *to the station*
   a la estación; *to the
   doctor* al médico
toast la tostada
tobacco el tabaco
tobacconist el estanco
today hoy
together juntos
toilet el váter
toilet paper el papel
   higiénico
tomato el tomate
tomato juice el zumo
   de tomate
tomorrow mañana
tongue la lengua
tonic la tónica
tonight esta noche
too (also) también;
   (excessively)
   demasiado
tooth el diente; *back
   tooth* la muela
toothache el dolor de
   muelas
toothbrush el cepillo
   de dientes
toothpaste la pasta
   dentífrica
tour la excursión
tourist el/la turista
tourist office la oficina
   de turismo
towel la toalla
tower la torre
town el pueblo
town hall
   el ayuntamiento
toy el juguete
trade fair la feria

tractor el tractor
traffic el tráfico
traffic jam el atasco
traffic lights el semáforo
trailer la caravana,
   el remolque
train el tren
trainee el aprendiz
translate traducir
translator el traductor/
   la traductora
trash can el contendor
   de basura, el cubo de
   la basura
travel agency la agencia
   de viajes
traveler's check
   el cheque de viaje
tray la bandeja
tree el árbol
truck el camión
trunk (car) el maletero
true cierto; *it's true* es
   verdad
try intentar
Tuesday martes
tunnel el túnel
turn (left/right) tuerza
   (a la izquierda/
   a la derecha)
turn: it's my turn me
   toca a mí
turn signal el
   intermitente
tweezers las pinzas
twelve doce
twenty veinte
two dos
typewriter la máquina
   de escribir

U

ugly feo
umbrella
   el paraguas
uncle el tío
under ... debajo de ...
underpants los
   calzoncillos
understand entender;
   I don't understand
   no entiendo
underwear la ropa
   interior
United States Estados
   Unidos
university
   la universidad
unleaded sin plomo
until hasta
unusual poco común
up arriba; (upward)
   hacia arriba
urgent urgente
us: it's for us es para
   nosotros/nosotras;
   give it to us dénoslo
use el uso; (verb) usar;
   it's no use no sirve
   de nada

useful útil
usual corriente
usually en general

V

vacancies (rooms)
   habitaciones libres
vacation las vacaciones
vaccination la vacuna
vacuum cleaner
   la aspiradora
valley el valle
valve la válvula
vanilla la vainilla
vase el jarrón
veal la (carne de)
   ternera
vegetables la verdura
vegetarian vegetariano
vehicle el vehículo
very muy; *very much*
   mucho
vest la camiseta
vet el veterinario
video (tape) la cinta de
   vídeo; (film) el vídeo
video games los vídeo-
   juegos
video recorder
   el (aparato de) vídeo
view la vista
viewfinder el visor de
   imagen
villa el chalet
village el pueblo
vinegar el vinagre
violin el violín
visit la visita; visitar
   (verb)
visiting hours las horas
   de visita
visitor el/la visitante
vitamin pills las
   vitaminas
vodka el vodka
voice la voz
voicemail la mensajería
   de voz

W

wait esperar; *wait!*
   ¡espere!
waiter el camarero;
   waiter! ¡camarero!
waiting room la sala
   de espera
waitress la camarera;
   waitress! ¡Oiga, por
   favor!
Wales Gales
walk (stroll) el paseo;
   (verb) andar; *to go for
   a walk* ir de paseo
wall la pared;
   (outside) el muro
wallet la cartera
want (verb) querer
war la guerra
wardrobe el armario

warm caliente;
  (weather) caluroso
was estaba/era
washing machine
  la zapatilla
wasp la avispa
watch el reloj; (verb)
  mirar
water el agua
waterfall la cascada
water heater
  el calentador (de agua)
wave la ola; (verb)
  agitar
wavy (hair) ondulado
we nosotros/nosotras
weather el tiempo
website la web site,
  el sitio web
wedding la boda
Wednesday miércoles
weeds las malas hierbas
week la semana
welcome (adj)
  bienvenido; (verb)
  dar la bienvenida;
  you're welcome
  no hay de qué
wellington boots
  las botas de agua
Welsh galés/galesa
were: you were
  (informal singular)
  eras/estabas; (formal
  singular) era/estaba;
  (informal plural)
  erais/estabais;
  (formal plural)
  eran/estaban; *we*
  were éramos/
  estábamos; *they were*
  eran/estaban
west el oeste
wet mojado

what? ¿qué?
wheel la rueda
wheelchair la silla de
  ruedas
when? ¿cuándo?
where? ¿dónde?
whether si
which? ¿cuál?
whiskey el whisky
white blanco
who? ¿quién?
why? ¿por qué?
wide ancho; *3 meters*
  wide de tres metros
  de anchura
wife la mujer
wind el viento
window la ventana
windshield el parabrisas
wine el vino
wine list la carta de
  vinos
wine merchant
  el vinatero
wing el ala
with con
without sin
witness el testigo
woman la mujer
wood (material)
  la madera
wool la lana
word la palabra
work el trabajo; (verb)
  trabajar; (to
  function) funcionar
worse peor
worst (el) peor
wrapping paper
  el papel de envolver;
  (for presents)
  el papel de regalo
wrench la llave inglesa
wrist la muñeca

writing paper el papel
  de escribir
wrong equivocado

X, Y, Z

X-ray department
  el servicio de
  radiología
year el año
yellow amarillo
yes sí
yesterday ayer
yet todavía; *not yet*
  todavía no
yogurt el yogur
you (informal
  singular) tú; (formal
  singular) usted;
  (informal plural,
  m/f) vosotros/
  vosotras; (formal
  plural) ustedes
young joven
your: your book
  (informal singular)
  tu libro; (formal
  singular) su libro;
  your shoes (informal
  singular) tus zapatos;
  (formal singular)
  sus zapato
yours: is this yours?
  (informal) ¿es tuyo
  esto?; (formal) ¿es suyo
  esto?
youth hostel el albergue
  juvenil
ZIP code el código
  postal *zipper* la
  cremallera
zoo el zoo

Dictionary
Spanish *to English*

The gender of Spanish nouns listed here is indicated by the abbreviations "(m)" and "(f)," for masculine and feminine. Plural nouns are followed by the abbreviations "(m pl)" or "(f pl)." Spanish adjectives (adj) vary according to the gender and number of the word they describe, and the masculine form is shown here. In general, adjectives that end in **-o** adopt an **-a** ending in the feminine form, and those that end in **-e** usually stay the same. For the plural form, an **-s** is added.

A

a *to*; a América *to America*; a la estación *to the station*; al médico *to the doctor*; a las tres *at 3 o'clock*

abanico (m) *fan (handheld)*

abierto *open* (adj)

abogado/abogada (m/f) *lawyer*

abrebotellas (m) *bottle opener*

abrelatas (m) *can opener*

abrigo (m) *coat*

abril *April*

abrir *to open*

abuela (f) *grandmother*

abuelo (m) *grandfather*

abuelos (m pl) *grandparents*

aburrido *boring*

acaba de llegar *it's just arrived*

accidente (m) *accident*

aceite (m) *oil*; el aceite de oliva *olive oil*

aceituna (f) *olive*

acelerador (m) *accelerator*

acera (f) *pavement*

acondicionador (m) *conditioner (hair)*

acuerdo: me acuerdo *I remember*; no me acuerdo *I don't remember*

adaptador (m) *adapter*

adelantar *pass (car)*

adiós *goodbye*

aduana (f) *customs*

aerodeslizador (m) *hovercraft*

aeropuerto (m) *airport*

afeitado (m) *shave*; afeitarse *to shave*

after-shave (m) *aftershave*

afueras (f pl) *suburbs*

agencia (f) *agency*

agencia de viajes (f) *travel agency*

agenda (f) *planner*

agitar *to wave*

agosto *August*

agradable *pleasant*

agradecer *to thank*

agua (m) *water*; el agua con gas *sparkling water*; el agua mineral *mineral water*; el agua potable *drinking water*; el agua sin gas *still water*

aguja (f) *needle*

ahora *now*; ¿y ahora qué? *what next?*

aire (m) *air*

aire acondicionado (m) *air conditioning*

ajedrez (m) *chess*

ajo (m) *garlic*

ajustado *tight*

ala (m) *wing*

albañil (m) *handyman, builder*

albaricoque (m) *apricot*

albergue juvenil (m) *youth hostel*

alcachofa (f) *artichoke*

alcohol (m) *alcohol*

alegre *glad*

alemán *German*

Alemania *Germany*

alérgico *allergic*

alfiler (m) *pin*

alfombra (f) *carpet; rug*

algo *something*

algodón (m) *cotton, cotton balls*

alguien *somebody*

alguna: en alguna parte *somewhere*

allí *there, over there*

almohada (f) *pillow*

alojamiento (m) *accommodation*

alquilar *to rent*

alto *high, tall, loud*

¡alto! *stop!*

amante (m/f) *lover*

amargo *bitter*

amarillo *yellow*

ambulancia (f) *ambulance*

América *America*

americano/americana (m/f) *American*

amigo/amiga (m/f) *friend*; amigo/amiga por correspondencia (m/f) *pen pal*

amontillado *medium (sherry)*

amor (m) *love*

ampliación (f) *enlargement*

ampolla (f) *blister*

análisis de sangre (m) *blood test*

andar *to walk*

andén (m) *platform*

anfiteatro (m) *lecture theater*

anfitriona (f) *hostess*

anillo (m) *ring (jewelry)*

animal (m) *animal*; los animales de compañía/los animales domésticos *pets*

año (m) *year*

antes de ... *before ...*

anticonceptivo (m) *contraceptive*

anticongelante (m) *antifreeze*

anticuario (m) *antique shop*

antiséptico (m) *antiseptic*

aparcamiento (m) *parking lot*

aparcar *to park*; prohibido aparcar *no parking*

apartamento (m) *apartment*

apellido (m) *surname*

aperitivo (m) *aperitif*

apetito (m) *appetite*

aprender *learn*

aprendiz (m) *trainee*

apretón de manos (m) *handshake*

araña (f) *spider*

árbol (m) *tree*

árbol de levas (m) *camshaft*

arcón (m) *chest (furniture)*

arena (f) *sand*

Argelia *Algeria*

armario (m) *cupboard, wardrobe*

arreglar *repair*

arriba *up*; hacia arriba *upward*

arroyo (m) *stream (small river)*

arroz (m) *rice*

arte (m) *art*

artículos de punto (m pl) *knitwear*

artista (m/f) *artist*

asado *roasted*

ascensor (m) *lift*

asiento (m) *seat*; el asiento infantil *car seat (for a baby/child)*

asistenta (f) *cleaner*

asmático *asthmatic*

aspiradora (f) *vacuum cleaner*

aspirina (f) *aspirin*

atar *to tie*

atasco (m) *traffic jam*

aterrizar *to land*

ático (m) *attic*

atractivo *attractive (offer)*

audífono (m) *hearing aid*

auriculares (m pl) *headphones*

Australia *Australia*

australiano/australiana (m/f) *Australian*

autobús (m) *bus*; autobús del aeropuerto *airport bus*

autocaravana (f) *camper van*

automático *automatic*

autónomo/autónoma (m/f) *self-employed*

autopista (f) *expressway*

avería (f) (car) *breakdown*; he tenido una avería *I've had a breakdown*

aves (f pl) *poultry*

avión (m) *aircraft*

avispa (f) *wasp*

ayer *yesterday*

ayuda (f) *help*

ayudar *to help*

ayuntamiento (m) *town hall*

azúcar (m) *sugar*

azul *blue*

B

bacon (m) *bacon*

bailar *to dance*

baile (m) *dance*

bajarse *to get off (bus, etc.)* ; *to get out*

bajo *low, short*

balandro (m) *sailboat*

balcón (m) *balcony*

Baleares: las (Islas) Baleares *Balearic Islands*

balón (m) *soccer (ball)*; el balón de playa *beach ball*

baloncesto (m) *basketball*

bañador (m) *swimsuit, swimming trunks*

banco (m) *bank*

banda (f) *band (musicians)*

bandeja (f) *tray*

bandera (f) *flag*

baño (m) *bathtub, bathroom*; darse un baño *to take a bath*; el traje de baño *swimsuit*

bar (m) *bar (drinks)*

baraja (f) *deck of cards*

barato *inexpensive*

barba (f) *beard*

barbacoa (f) *barbecue*

barca (f) *small boat*; la barca de remos *rowing boat*

barco (m) *boat, ship*

barra de labios (f) *lipstick*

bastante *enough, quite, fairly*

basura (f) *litter, garbage*

batería (f) *battery (car)*

bebé (m) *baby*

beber *to drink*; ¿quiere beber algo? *would you like something to drink?*

bebida (f) *drink*

beige *beige*

beneficios (m pl) *profits*

berenjenas (f pl) *eggplant*

biblioteca (f) *library*

bicicleta (f) *bicycle*; la bicicleta de montaña *mountain bike*

bien *good*; te sienta bien *it suits you*

bienvenido *welcome*

bigote (m) *mustache*

billete (m) *fare, ticket (train, etc.)*; billete de ida y vuelta (m) *round-trip ticket*

billete de banco (m) *banknote*

bizcocho (m) *sponge cake*

blanco *white*

blando *soft*

bloc (m) *notepad*

bloque de oficinas (m) *office block*

blusa (f) *blouse*

boca (f) *mouth*

bocadillo (m) *sandwich*

boda (f) *wedding*

bodega (f) *basement*

bolígrafo (m) *ballpoint pen*

bollo (m) *roll (bread)*

bolsa (f) *bag, packet (candy, chips)*; la bolsa de basura *garbage bag*; la bolsa de plástico *plastic bag*

bolsillo (m) *pocket*

bolso (m) *handbag*

bombilla (f) *light bulb*

bonito *nice, pretty, attractive (object)*

bordado (m) *embroidery*

borde (m) *edge, border, side*

borracho *drunk*

bosque (m) *forest*

bota (f) *boot*

botas de agua (f pl) *wellington boots*

botella (f) *bottle*

botón (m) *button*

brazo (m) *arm*

bridge (m) *bridge (game)*

británico/británica (m/f) *British*

brocha (f) *paint brush*

broche (m) *brooch*

broma (f) *joke*

bronceado *suntanned*

broncearse *suntan: to get a suntan*

buenas noches *good evening*

buenas tardes *good afternoon*

bueno *good, good to eat, tasty*

buenos días *good morning*

bufanda (f) *scarf*

buzón (m) *mailbox*

C

cabeza (f) *head*

cabina telefónica (f) *phone booth*

cable alargador (m) *extension cord*

cacahuetes (m pl) *peanuts*

cada *every, each*; viente euros cada uno *20 euros each*

café (m) *café, coffee;*
el café con leche
coffee with milk; el
café instantáneo
instant coffee; el café
solo *espresso*

caja (f) *box; checkout;*
la caja de bombones
box of chocolates;
la caja de cambios
gearbox

cajero (m) *cashier;*
el cajero automático
ATM

cajetilla (f) *packet*
(cigarettes)

calambre (m) *cramp*

calcetines (m pl) *socks*

calculadora (m)
calculator

calefacción (f) *heating;*
la calefacción central
central heating

calentador (de agua)
(m) *water heater*

calidad (f) *quality*

caliente *warm*

callado *quiet* (person)

calle (f) *street;* la calle
principal *main road*

caluroso *warm*
(weather)

calzoncillos (m pl)
underpants

cama (f) *bed*

cámara de fotos (f)
camera

cámara neumática (f)
inner tube

camarera (f) *waitress*

camarero (m) *waiter;*
¡camarero! *waiter!*

cambiar *to change*
(money)

cambiarse *to change*
(clothes)

cambio (m) *change*
(money); *exchange
rate*

camino (m) *path*

camión (m) *truck*

camisa (f) *shirt*

camiseta (f) *vest*

camisón (m)
nightgown

campana (f) *bell*
(church)

camping (m)
campground

camping-gas (m) *stove
fuel*

campo (m) *countryside,
field*

Canadá *Canada*

canadiense *Canadian*

canal (m) *canal*

Canarias: las (Islas)
Canarias *Canaries*

canción (f) *song*

candado (m) *padlock*

cangrejo (m) *crab*

cansado *tired*

cantar *to sing*

capazo (m) *crib*

capó (m) *hood* (car)

cara (f) *face*

caramelos (m) *candy*

caravana (f) *trailer*

carburador (m)
carburetor

cardenal (m) *bruise*

cargador (m) *charger*

carne (f) *meat*

carne de cerdo (f) *pork*

carne de vaca (f) *beef*

carnet de conducir (m)
driver's license

carnicería (f) *butcher
shop*

caro *expensive*

carpintero (m)
carpenter

carretera (f) *road*

carrito (m) *cart*

carta (f) *letter* (mail);
menu; la carta de
vinos (f) *wine list*

cartera (f) *purse,
briefcase, wallet*

carterista (m)
pickpocket

cartero (m) *mail
carrier*

casa (f) *house, home;*
en casa *at home*

casado *married*

cascada (f) *waterfall*

casi *almost*

cassette (f) *cassette*

castaño *brown* (hair)

castañuelas (f pl)
castanets

castellano *Castilian*

Castilla *Castile*

castillo (m) *castle*

Cataluña *Catalonia*

catedral (f) *cathedral*

catedrático (m)
professor

católico *Catholic* (adj)

catorce *fourteen*

cazo (m) *saucepan*

cebo (m) *bait*

cebolla (f) *onion*

ceja (f) *eyebrow*

cementerio (m)
cemetery

cena (f) *dinner, supper,
dinner party*

cenicero (m) *ashtray*

centro (m) *center;
downtown;* el centro
deportivo *gym;* en el
centro *middle: in the
middle*

cepillar el pelo *to brush
hair*

cepillo (m) *brush* (for
cleaning); el cepillo
del pelo *hair brush;*
el cepillo de dientes
toothbrush

cerca *near, close;* (f)
fence

cereza (f) *cherry*

cerilla (f) *match* (light)

cerrado *closed*

cerrar *to close*

cerrojo (m) *bolt* (on
door)

certificado (m)
certificate

cerveza (f) *beer*

césped (m) *lawn*

cesto (m) *basket*

chal (m) *shawl*

chalet (m) *villa*

champiñones (m pl)
mushrooms

champú (m) *shampoo*

chandal (m) *jogging
suit*

chaparrón (m) *shower*
(rain)

chaqueta (f) *jacket*

charcutería (f)
delicatessen

charla (f) *talk*

cheque (m) *check;*
el cheque de viaje
traveler's check

chica (f) *girl*

chicle (m) *chewing gum*

chico (m) *boy*

chimenea (f) *chimney,
fireplace*

chincheta (f) *drawing
pin*

chiste (m) *joke* (funny
story)

chocolate (m)
chocolate

chuleta (f) *chop* (food)

chupa-chups (m)
lollipop

ciclismo (m) *cycling*

ciclomotor (m) *moped*

ciego *blind* (cannot
see)

cielo (m) *sky*

cien *hundred*

ciencias (f pl) *science*

cierto *true*

cigalas (f pl) *crayfish*

cigarrillo (m) *cigarette*

cinco *five*

cincuenta *fifty*

cine (m) *movie theater*

cinta (f) *cassette;* el cinta
de vídeo *video tape*

cinturón (m) *belt;* el
cinturón de seguridad
seat belt

cita (f) *appointment*

ciudad (f) *city, town;*
el centro ciudad
downtown

claro *clear* (water);
light (adj: not dark)

clase (f) *class; lesson*

clavo (m) *nail* (metal)

claxon (m) *horn* (car)

cliente (m) *client*

cobrador (m) *conductor (bus)*

cobrar *to cash*

cocer *to cook, boil*

cocer al horno *to bake*

coche (m) *car*

coche-cama (m) *sleeper car*

cochecito (m) *baby carriage*

cocina (f) *stove; kitchen*

cocinero/cocinera (m/f) *cook*

coctel (m) *cocktail party*

código *code*; el código de la circulación *highway code*; el código postal *ZIP code*

codo (m) *elbow*

coger *catch*; coger el tren *to catch the train*

cojín (m) *cushion*

col (f) *cabbage*

cola (f) *line*

colada (f) *laundry (washed)*

colcha (f) *bedspread*

colchón (m) *mattress*

colchoneta (f) *air mattress*

colección (f) *collection (stamps, etc.)*

coliflor (f) *cauliflower*

collar (m) *collar (of animal)*

collar (m) *necklace; color*

combinacíon (f) *slip (underwear)*

comedor (m) *dining room*

comer *to eat*

comida (f) *food, meal; lunch*

comida ligera (f) *snack*

comisaría (f) *police station*

como *like*; como éste *like this one*

¿cómo? *how?*; ¿cómo se llama usted? *what's your name?*¿cómo dice? *pardon?*, *what did you say?*

cómoda (f) *chest of drawers*

compañía aérea (f) *airline*

compartimento (m) *compartment*

completamente *completely*

complicado *complicated*

compra (f) *shopping*

comprar *to buy*

comprendo *I see*

compresas (f pl) *sanitary napkins*

con *with*

coñac (m) *brandy*

concha (f) *shell*

concierto (m) *concert*

concurrido *crowded*

condón (m) *condom*

conducir *to drive*

conductor (m) *driver*

conejo (m) *rabbit*

conferencia (f) *conference*; la sala de conferencias *conference room*

congelador (m) *freezer*

congelados (m pl) *frozen foods*

conocer *to know (person, place)*

conserje (m) *porter (hotel)*

consulado (m) *consulate*

contable (m/f) *accountant*

contendor de basura (m) *trash can*

contento *happy*

contestador automático (m) *answering machine*

contra *against*

contraseña (f) *password*

contrato (m) *contract*

copa (f) *glass (for drinking)*

corazón (m) *heart*

corazones (m pl) *hearts (cards)*

corbata (f) *tie*

corcho (m) *cork*

cordero (m) *lamb*

cordones (de los zapatos) (m pl) *(shoe)laces*

correa (f) *leash*

correcto *right (correct)*

correo (m) *mail*; el correo certificado *registered mail*; el correo electrónico *email*

Correos: (la oficina de) Correos (f) *post office*

correr *to run*

corrida de toros (f) *bullfight*

corriente *ordinary; usual*

cortadura (f) *cut*

cortar *to chop, cut*

cortauñas (m) *nail clippers*

corte de pelo (m) *haircut*

cortina (f) *curtain*

corto *short*

coser *to sew*

cosméticos (m pl) *cosmetics*

costar *to cost*; ¿cuánto cuesta? *what does it cost?*

crema (f) *cream (lotion)*

crema de zapatos (f) *shoe polish*

cremallera (f) *zip*

creo que ... *I think that ...*

crepes (f pl) *pancakes*

crisis nerviosa (f) *nervous breakdown*

cristal (m) *glass (material)*

crucero (m) *cruise*

cuaderno (m) *notebook*

cuadrado *square (adj)*

¿cuál? *which?*

cualquiera de ellos *either of them*

¿cuándo? *when?*

¿cuánto cuesta? *what does it cost?, how much is it?*

¿cuántos años tiene? *how old are you?*

cuarenta *forty*

cuarto (m) *quarter, room; (adj) fourth*

cuarto de baño (m) *bathroom*

cuarto de estar (m) *living room, lounge*

cuatro *four*

cubo (m) *bucket*; el cubo de la basura *trash can*

cucaracha (f) *cockroach*

cuchara (f) *spoon*

cuchillas de afeitar (f pl) *razor blades*

cuchillo (m) *knife*

cuello (m) *neck, collar*

cuenco (m) *bowl*

cuenta (f) *bill*

cuerda (f) *string; rope*

cuerno (m) *horn (animal)*

cuero (m) *leather*

cuerpo (m) *body*

cueva (f) *cave*

¡cuidado! *be careful!*

cumpleaños (m) *birthday*

cuna (f) *crib*

cura (m) *priest*

curry (m) *curry*

D

dar *give*; dar la bienvenida *to welcome*

de *of*; de algún modo *somehow*; de ida *single (ticket)*

debajo de *below, under*

decir *say*; ¿qué ha dicho? *what did you say?*; ¿cómo se dice ...? *how do you say ...?*

declaración (f) *statement*

dedo (m) *finger*

delante de *in front of*
...delgado *thin*
demasiado *too (excessively)*
démelo *give it to me*
dentadura postiza (f) *dentures, false teeth*
dentista (m/f) *dentist*
denuncia (f) *police report*
departemento (m) *department*
deporte (m) *sports*
derecho *law, justice;* no hay derecho *it's not fair;* (adj) *right (not left)*
desayuno (m) *breakfast*
descansar *to rest*
descuento (m) *discount*
desmayarse *to faint*
desodorante (m) *deodorant*
despacho (m) *office (room)*
despegue (m) *take off*
despertador (m) *alarm clock*
después *then (after);* después de ... *after ...*
destornillador (m) *screwdriver*
detergente (m) *laundry detergent*
detrás de ... *behind ...*
devolver *to return (give back); to be sick (vomit)*
día (m) *day;* el día de fiesta *public holiday*
diabético *diabetic*
diamantes (m pl) *diamonds*
diarrea (f) *diarrhea*
diccionario (m) *dictionary*
diciembre *December*
diecinueve *nineteen*
dieciocho *eighteen*
dieciséis *sixteen*
diecisiete *seventeen*
diente (m) *tooth*
diesel *diesel* (adj: engine)
diez *ten*
diferente *different*
difícil *difficult*
dígame *hello (on phone)*
dinero (m) *money, cash;* no tengo dinero *I have no money*
dirección (f) *address*
director/directora (m/f) *manager (hotel); conductor (orchestra)*
disco (m) *record (music)*
disco compacto (m) *CD*
discoteca (f) *nightclub*
diseñador/diseñadora (m/f) *designer*

disponible *available*
distancia *distance;* ¿qué distancia hay a ...? *how far is it to ...?*
distinto *separate, different* (adj); ¡eso es distinto! *that's different!;* quería otro distinto *I'd like a different one*
diversiones (f pl) *entertainment*
divertido; (odd) raro *funny*
divorciado *divorced*
doce *twelve*
documento (m) *document*
dólar (m) *dollar*
dolor (m) *ache, pain;* el dolor de cabeza *headache;* el dolor de estómago *stomach-ache;* el dolor de muelas *toothache*
domingo *Sunday*
¿dónde? *where?;* ¿dónde está ...? *where is ...?*
dónut (m) *doughnut*
dormir *to sleep*
dormitorio (m) *bedroom*
dos *two;* los dos *both*
ducha (f) *shower (bath)*
dulce *sweet* (adj: not sour)
dunas (f pl) *sand dunes*
durante *during*
duro *hard (not soft)*
duty-free (m) *duty-free shop*

E

echar al correo *to mail*
echar el cerrojo *to bolt*
edificio (m) *building*
edredón (m) *comforter*
eje (m) *axle*
ejecutivo (m) *executive*
ejemplo (m) *example;* por ejemplo *for example*
él *he, him, the* (m); es para él *it's for him*
elástico *elastic*
electricidad (f) *electricity*
electricista (m/f) *electrician*
eléctrico *electric*
ella *she, her, the* (f); es para ella *it's for her*
ellos/ellas *they, them;* es para ellos/ellas *it's for them*
email (m) *email;* la dirección de email *email address*
embajada (f) *embassy*
embarazada *pregnant*

embarazoso *embarrassing*
emergencia (f) *emergency*
empaste (m) *filling (in tooth)*
empezar *to start*
empleado (m) *employee*
empujar *to push*
en *on, at, in;* en inglés *in English;* en el hotel *in the hotel;* en Barcelona *in Barcelona;* en Correos *at the post office;* en su casa *at your place*
encaje (m) *lace*
encantado/encantada (m/f) *pleased to meet you*
encargado (m) *caretaker*
encendedor (m) *lighter*
encendido (m) *ignition*
enchufe (m) *plug (electrical)*
encima de ... *over ...*
encuentro (m) *meeting;* no me encuentro bien *I don't feel well*
enero *January*
enfermo/enferma (m/f) *nurse*
enfrente de *across from;* enfrente del hotel *across from the hotel*
¡enhorabuena! *congratulations!*
ensalada (f) *salad*
entender *to understand;* no entiendo *I don't understand*
entonces *then, so*
entrada (f) *entrance, ticket (theater, etc.)*
entrantes (m pl) *starters*
entre ... *between ...*
entrega (f) *delivery*
enviar por fax *to fax*
epiléptico *epileptic*
equipaje (m) *luggage;* el equipaje de mano *carry-on luggage*
equipo de música (m) *music system*
equivocación (f) *mistake*
equivocado *wrong*
era *you were* (formal): *it/he/she was*
éramos *we were*
eran *they were*
eras *you were (informal)*
eres *you are (informal)*
es *you are* (formal)
es *it/he/she was*
escalera (f) *staircase;* la escalera mecánica *escalator;* las escaleras *stairs*
escarcha (f) *frost*

escocés/escocesa (m/f) *Scottish*

Escocia *Scotland*

escopeta (f) *gun* (rifle)

escuela (f) *school*

ese/esa *that*; ese autobús *that bus*; ese hombre *that man*; esa mujer *that woman*; ¿qué es eso? *what's that?*

ése/ésa *that, that one*; esmalte de uñas (m) *nail polish*

esos/esas *those, those ones*; esos hombres *those men*; esas mujeres *those women*

espalda (f) *back* (body)

España *Spain*

español/española (m/f) *Spanish, Spaniard*

especialidad (f) *field of study*

espejo (m) *mirror*

esperar *to wait*; ¡espere! *wait!*

espinacas (f pl) *spinach*

espuma de afeitar (f) *shaving foam*

espuma moldeadora (f) *mousse* (for hair)

esquina (f) *corner* (of street)

esquís (m pl) *skis*

está *you are* (formal)

está *it/he/she is*

esta noche *tonight*

estaba *it/he/she was; you were* (formal)

estábamos *we were*

estaban *they were*

estabas *you were* (informal)

estaca (f) *tent peg*

estación (f) *station*; la estación de autobuses *bus station*; la estación de esquí *ski resort*; la estación de metro *metro station*

Estados Unidos *United States*

estamos *we are*

están *they are*

estanco (m) *tobacconist*

estaquilla (f) *tent peg*

estás *you are* (informal)

estatua (f) *statue*

este *east*; el Este *the East*

éste/ésta *this, this one*; este hombre *this man*; esta mujer *this woman*; ¿qué es esto? *what's this?*; éste es el señor ... *this is Mr. ...*

estómago (m) *stomach*

estos/estas *these, these ones*; estos hombres *these men*; estas

mujeres *these women*; éstos son míos *these are mine*

estoy *I am*

estrecho *narrow* (adj)

estrella (f) *star*

estudiante (m/f) *student*

estufa (f) *heater*

estúpido *stupid*

etiqueta (f) *label*

evidente *clear* (obvious)

excelente *excellent*

exceso de equipaje (m) *excess baggage*

excursión (f) *excursion, tour*

exposición (f) *exhibition*

externa *external*

extintor (m) *fire extinguisher*

extranjero/extranjera (m/f) *foreigner*

F

fácil *easy*

factor de protección (m) *protection factor (SPF)*

factura (f) *invoice*

facturación (f) *check-in*

facturar *to check in*

falda (f) *skirt*

falta: no hace falta *there's no need*

familia (f) *family*

fan (m) *fan* (enthusiast)

fantástico *fantastic*

farmacia (f) *pharmacy*

faros (m pl) *headlights*

fax (m) *fax*

febrero *February*

¡felicidades! *happy birthday!*

feliz *happy*

feo *ugly*

feria (f) *fair, trade fair*

ferretería (f) *hardware store*

ferrocarril (m) *railroad*

ferry (m) *ferry*

fiebre (f) *temperature, fever*; la fiebre del heno *hay fever*

fiesta (f) *party* (celebration)

filete (m) *steak*

filtro (m) *filter*

fin (m) *end*; ¡por fin! *at last!*

final (m) *end*

fino *dry* (sherry)

flash (m) *flash* (camera)

flauta (f) *flute*

flequillo (m) *bangs* (hair)

flexo (m) *swing-armlamp*

flor (f) *flower*

folleto (m) *brochure, leaflet*

fonda (f) *inn*

fondo (m) *bottom*

fontanero/fontanera (m/f) *plumber*

foto(grafía) (f) *photograph*

fotocopiadora (f) *photocopier*

fotografiar *to photograph*

fotógrafo (m) *photographer*

fotómetro (m) *light meter*

frambuesa (f) *raspberry*

francés *French*

Francia *France*

fregadero (m) *sink*

freír *to fry*

frenar *to brake*

freno (m) *brake*; el freno de emergencia *emergency brake*; el freno de mano *handbrake*

fresas (f pl) *strawberries*

fresco *cool*

frigorífico (m) *refrigerator*

frío *cold* (adj); I'm cold tengo frío

frito *fried*

frontera (f) *border* (between countries)

fruta (f) *fruit*

fuego (m) *fire*; los fuegos artificiales *fireworks*

fuel-oil *diesel* (oil)

fuente (f) *fountain*

fuera *outside*

fuerte *strong*

fumar *to smoke*

funcionar *to work* (function)

fútbol (m) *soccer* (game)

G

gabardina (f) *raincoat*

gafas (f pl) *glasses*; las gafas de sol *sunglasses*

galería de arte (f) *art gallery*

Gales *Wales*

galés/galesa *Welsh*

galleta (f) *cookie*

gambas (f pl) *shrimp*

ganga (f) *bargain*

garage (m) *garage* (for parking)

garantía (f) *guarantee*

garantizar *to guarantee*

garganta (f) *throat*

gas para el encendedor (m) *lighter fuel*

gasolina (f) *gasoline*

gasolinera (f) *gas station*

gato (m) *cat*

gay *gay* (homosexual)

gel (m) *gel* (hair); el gel de ducha *shower gel*

gemelos (m pl) *cuff links*

general: en general *usually*

gente (f) *people*

gerente (m/f) *manager*

Gibraltar *Gibraltar*

ginebra (f) *gin*

gobierno (m) *government*

Golfo de Vizcaya (m) *Bay of Biscay*

goma (f) *rubber band*; *rubber* (material)

goma de borrar (f) *eraser*

gordo *fat* (adj)

gorra (f) *cap* (hat)

gorro (m) *woollen hat*

gotas (f pl) *drops*

gracias *thank you*

Gran Bretaña *Great Britain*

grande *big, large*

grandes almacenes (m pl) *department store*

granja (f) *farm*

granjero (m) *farmer*

grapadora (f) *stapler*

grasa (f) *fat* (meat, etc.)

gratis *free* (no charge)

grifo (m) *faucet*

gris *gray*

gritar *to shout*

grosellas negras (f pl) *black currants*

grueso *thick*

grupo (m) *party* (group)

guantes (m pl) *gloves*

guapo *attractive, beautiful, handsome* (person)

guerra (f) *war*

guía (m/f) *guide*; la guía telefónica *phone book*; la guía turística *guide book*

guisantes (m pl) *peas*

guisar *to cook*

guitarra (f) *guitar*

gustar *like*: me gusta ... *I like ...*; me gusta nadar *I like swimming*

H

habitación (f) *room*; la habitación doble *double room*; la habitación individual *single room*; habitaciones libres *vacancies*

hablar *to talk*; ¿habla ...? *do you speak ...?*;

no hablo ... *I don't speak ...*

hacer *to do, make*; hacer auto-stop *to hitchhike*; hacer footing *to jog*; hacer punto *to knit*; hacer transbordo *to change* (trains, etc.); hace sol *it's sunny*

hacha (m) *axe*

hacia abajo *down*

hambre *hungry*; tengo hambre *I'm hungry*

hamburguesa (f) *hamburger*

hámster (m) *hamster*

harina (f) *flour*

hasta *until*

hay... *there is/are...* ; ¿hay ...? *is/are there ...?*

helado (m) *ice cream*

hepatitis (f) *hepatitis*

herida (f) *injury*

hermana (f) *sister*

hermano (m) *brother*

hervido *boiled*

hervidor de agua (m) *teakettle*

hervir *to boil* (water)

hidroaleta (f) *hydrofoil*

hielo (m) *ice*

hierba (f) *grass*

hierro (m) *iron* (material)

hígado (m) *liver*

higo (m) *fig*

hija (f) *daughter*

hijastra (f) *stepdaughter*

hijastro (m) *stepson*

hijo (m) *son*

hincha (m) *soccer fan*

historia (f) *history*

hobby (m) *hobby*

hoguera (f) *campfire*

hoja (f) *leaf, sheet* (of paper)

hojalata (f) *tin*

hola *hello*

hombre (m) *man*

hombro (m) *shoulder*

homeopatía (f) *homeopathy*

honrado *honest*

hora (f) *hour*; ¿qué hora es? *what's the time?*

horario (m) *schedule*; el horario de apertura *opening times*

horca (f) *garden fork*

horno (m) *oven*

horrible *awful, horrible*

hospital (m) *hospital*

hoy *today*

hueso (m) *bone*

huevo (m) *egg*

húmedo *damp*

humo (m) *smoke*

I

idioma (m) *language*

iglesia (f) *church*

imperdible (m) *safety pin*

imposible *impossible*

impreso de solicitud (m) *application form*

impresora (f) *printer*

incendio (m) *fire* (blaze)

incluido *included*

indigestión *indigestion*

infección (f) *infection*

información (f) *information*

informe (m) *report*

ingeniería (f) *engineering*

Inglaterra *England*

inglés/inglesa *English*

inhalador (m) *inhaler* (for asthma, etc.)

inmediatamente *immediately*

insecto (m) *insect*

insolación (f) *sunstroke*

insomnio (m) *insomnia*

instrumento musical (m) *musical instrument*

intentar *to try*

interesante *interesting*

intermitente (m) *turn signal*

internet (m) *Internet*

interpretar *to interpret*

intérprete (m/f) *interpreter*

interruptor (m) *switch*

intoxicación alimenticia (f) *food poisoning*

invitación (f) *invitation*

invitada (f) *guest*

inyección (f) *injection*

ir *to go*; ir a esquiar *to go skiing*; ir de compras *to go shopping*

Irlanda *Ireland*; Irlanda del Norte *Northern Ireland*

irlandés/irlandesa *Irish*

isla (f) *island*

Italia *Italy*

italiano/italiana (m/f) *Italian*

izquierdo *left* (not right)

J

jabón (m) *soap*; el jabón de lavadora *laundry detergent*

jamón (m) *ham*

jarabe (m) *syrup*

jardín (m) *garden*

jarrita (f) *mug*

jarrón (m) *vase*

jaula (f) *cage*

jazz (m) *jazz*
jefe (m) *manager*
jengibre (m) *ginger* (spice)
jerez (m) *sherry*
jeringuilla (f) *syringe*
jersey (m) *sweater*
joven *young*
joyería (f) *jeweler*
judías (f pl) *beans*
jueves *Thursday*
jugar *to play*
juguete (m) *toy*
julio *July*
junio *June*
junto a *near*; junto a la puerta *near the door*; junto a la ventana *near the window*
juntos *together*

K, L

kilo (m) *kilo*
kilómetro (m) *kilometer*
kiosko de periódicos (m) *newsstand*
la (f) *the*
laca (f) *hairspray*
lado de (f) *beside*
ladrón (m) *thief*
lago (m) *lake*
lámpara (f) *lamp*
lamparilla de noche (f) *bedside lamp*
lana (f) *wool*
langosta (f) *lobster*
lápiz (m) *pencil*
largo *long*
las (f pl) *the*
lata (f) *can* (tin)
lavabo (m) *basin* (sink)
lavandería automática (f) *laundromat*
lavavajillas (m) *dishwasher*
laxante (m) *laxative*
leche (f) *milk*; la leche limpiadora *cleansing milk* (for skin)
lechuga (f) *lettuce*
leer *to read*
lejía *bleach*
lejos *far, far away*
lengua (f) *tongue*
lente (f) *lens*; las lentes de contacto *contact lenses*; las lentes de contacto semi-rígidas *gas-permeable lenses*
lento *slow*
letra (f) *letter* (of alphabet)
levantarse *to get up* (rise)
libra (f) *pound* (sterling)
libre *free* (not engaged)
libre de impuestos *duty-free*

libro (m) *book*; el libro de frases *phrase book*
licor (m) *liqueur*
ligero *light* (adj: not heavy)
lima (f) *lime* (fruit)
lima de uñas (f) *nailfile*
límite de velocidad (m) *speed limit*
limón (m) *lemon*
limonada (f) *lemonade*
limpio *clean* (adj)
línea (f) *line* (phone, etc.)
linterna (f) *flashlight*
listo *clever; ready*
literatura (f) *literature*
litro (m) *liter*
llamar por teléfono *to telephone*
llave (f) *key*; la llave de las tuercas *tire iron*; la llave inglesa *wrench*
llegar *to arrive*
lleno *crowded, full*; estoy lleno *I'm full*
llorar *to cry* (weep)
lluvia (f) *rain*
lo/la *it*
lo antes posible *as soon as possible*
loción (f); la loción anti-mosquitos *insect repellent lotion*; la loción bronceadora *suntan lotion*
loco *crazy*
lona impermeable (f) *groundsheet*
longitud (f) *length*
los (m pl) *the*
lo siento *I'm sorry*
luces de posición (f pl) *side lights*
lugar (m) *place, sight*; los lugares de interés de ... *the sights of ...*
luna (f) *moon*
lunes *Monday*
luz (f) *light*

M

madastra (f) *stepmother*
madera (f) *wood* (material)
madre (f) *mother*
maduro *ripe*
malas hierbas (f pl) *weeds*
maleta (f) *suitcase*
maletero (m) *trunk* (car)
Mallorca *Majorca*
malo *bad, poor* (quality)
mama *Mum*
mañana *tomorrow*
mañana (f) *morning*; por la mañana *in the morning*

mandar *to send*
mandarina (f) *tangerine*
manga (f) *sleeve*
mano (f) *hand*
manta (f) *blanket, rug*
mantequilla (f) *butter*
manzana (f) *apple*
mapa (m) *map*
maquillaje (m) *make-up*
maquina cortacésped (f) *lawn mower*
máquina de escribir (f) *typewriter*
máquina de fotos (f) *camera*
mar (m) *sea*
marea (f) *tide*
mareado *faint, dizzy*
margarina (f) *margarine*
marido (m) *husband*
mariscos (m pl) *seafood, shellfish*
mármol (m) *marble*
marrón *brown*
Marruecos *Morocco*
martes *Tuesday*
martillo (m) *hammer*
marzo *March*
más *more*; más de ... *more than ...* ; más tarde *later*; algo más *something else*; alguien más *someone else*
mástil (m) *tent pole*
matrícula (f) *license plate*
mayo *may*
mecánico (m) *mechanic*
media pensión *half board*
medianoche *midnight*
medias (f pl) *pantyhose, stockings*
medicina (f) *medicine*
médico/médica (m/f) *doctor*
medio *half*; media hora *half an hour*
mediodía (m) *noon*
Mediterráneo: el Mediterráneo *Mediterranean*
medusa (f) *jellyfish*
mejillones (m pl) *mussels*
mejor *best/better*
melocotón (m) *peach*
melón (m) *melon*
menos *less*
mensaje (m) *message*
mensajería de voz (f) *voicemail*
menú (del día) (m) *set menu*
menudo: a menudo *often*
mercado (m) *market*
mermelada (f) *jam*; la mermelada de naranja *marmalade*

mes (m) *month*

mesa (f) *table*; la mesa de escritorio *desk*

mesilla de noche (f) *nightstand*

metro (m) *subway*

mi(s) *my*; mi libro *my book*; mis llaves *my keys*

microondas (m) *microwave*

miel (f) *honey*

miércoles *Wednesday*

mil *thousand*

minusválido *disabled*

minuto (m) *minute*

mío *mine*; es mío *it's mine*

mirar *to watch*

misa (f) *mass* (church)

mismo *same*; el mismo vestido *the same dress*; la misma gente *the same people*; lo mismo otra vez, por favor *same again, please*

mochila (f) *backpack*

moda (f) *fashion*

modem (m) *modem*

mojado *wet*

moneda (f) *coin*

monedero (m) *purse*

monitor (m) *monitor*

montaña (f) *mountain*

monte (m) *hill*

monumento (m) *monument*

morado *purple*

moras (f pl) *blackberries*

mordedura (f) *bite* (dog)

morder *to bite* (dog)

morir *to die*

mosaico (m) *mosaic*

mosca (f) *fly* (insect)

mosquito (m) *mosquito*

mostaza (f) *mustard*

mostrador (m) *countertop*; el mostrador de facturación *check-in desk*

motocicleta (f) *motorcycle*

motor (m) *engine* (motor)

motora (f) *motorboat*

mover *to move* (something); moverse *move oneself*; ¡no se mueva! *don't move!*

mucho *much/many, a lot*; mucho mejor *much better*; mucho más despacio *much slower*; no muchos *not many*

mudarse (de casa) *to move* (house)

muebles (m pl) *furniture*

muela (f) *back tooth*

muelle (m) *dock*; *spring* (mechanical)

muerto *dead*

mujer (f) *woman, wife*

muletas (f pl) *crutches*

muñeca (f) *wrist*

muro (m) *wall* (outside)

museo (m) *museum*

música (f) *music*; la música clásica *classical music*; la música folklórica *folk music*; la música pop *pop music*

músico (m) *musician*

muy *very*

N

nací en ... *I was born in ...*

nada *nothing*; no queda nada *there's nothing left*; no sirve de nada *it's no use*

nadar *to swim*

nadie *nobody*

naranja (f) *orange* (fruit); *orange* (adj)

nariz (f) *nose*

nata (f) *cream* (dairy)

natación (f) *swimming*

náuseas *sick*; tengo náuseas *I feel sick*

navaja (f) *penknife*

navidad (f) *Christmas*

necesario *necessary*

necesito ... *I need ...*

negar *to deny*

negativo (m) *negative* (photo)

negocio (m) *business*

negro *black*

neozelandés/neozeland esa *New Zealander*

neumático (m) *tire*

ni ... ni ... *neither ... nor ...*

niebla (f) *fog*

nieta (f) *granddaughter*

nieto (m) *grandson*

nieve (f) *snow*

ninguno/ninguna: ninguno de ellos *neither of them*; en ninguna parte *nowhere*

niño/niña *child* (m/f); los niños *children*; el niño pequeño *baby*

no *no* (response), *not*; no hay de qué *you're welcome*; no importa *it doesn't matter*; no es/está ... *(s)he's not ...*

noche (f) *night*

nombre (m) *name*; el nombre de pila *first name*

norte (m) *north*

nosotros/nosotras *we, us*; es para nosotros/ nosotras *it's for us*

noticias (f pl) *news*

novela (f) *novel*

noventa *ninety*

novia (f) *girlfriend*

noviembre *November*

novio (m) *boyfriend*

nudista (m/f) *nudist*

nuestro *our*; es nuestro *it's ours*

Nueva Zelanda *New Zealand*

nueve *nine*

nuevo *new*

nuez (f) *nut* (fruit)

número (m) *number*; los números *figures*

nunca *never*

O

o *or*; o bien ... o ... *either ... or ...*

obra de teatro (f) *play* (theater)

obturador (m) *shutter* (camera)

Océano Atlántico (m) *Atlantic Ocean*

ochenta *eighty*

ocho *eight*

octubre *October*

oculista (m/f) *optician*

ocupado *busy* (phone); *occupied*

oeste (m) *west*

oficina (f) *office* (place); *branch* (of company); la oficina de objetos perdidos *lost property office*; la oficina de turismo *tourist office*

oído (m) *(inner) ear*

¡oiga, por favor! *excuse me!* (to get attention); *waiter/waitress!*

oír *to hear*

ojo (m) *eye*

ola (f) *wave*

oler *to smell*

olivo (m) *olive tree*

olor (m) *smell*

oloroso *sweet* (sherry)

olvidar *to forget*

once *eleven*

ondulado *wavy* (hair)

operación (f) *operation*

operadora (f) *operator*

oporto (m) *port* (drink)

orden del día (m) *agenda*

ordenador (m) *computer*

oreja *ear* (f)

órgano (m) *organ* (music)

oro (m) *gold*

orquesta (f) *orchestra*

oscuro *dark*; azul oscuro *dark blue*

ostra (f) *oyster*

otra vez *again*

otro *another; other*; el otro *the other one*; en otro sitio *somewhere else*

P

padastro (m) *stepfather*

padre (m) *father*; los padres *parents*

pagar *to pay*; pagar al contado *to pay cash*

página (f) *page*

pago (m) *payment*

país (m) *country* (state)

pájaro (m) *bird*

pala (f) *spade*

palabra (f) *word*

palacio (m) *palace*

palanca de velocidades (f) *gear stick*

pálido *pale*

pan (m) *bread*

panadería (f) *bread shop*

pañal (m) *diaper*; los pañales desechables *disposable diapers*

paño de cocina (m) *dish cloth*

pantalla (f) *lampshade, screen*

pantalón (m) *pants, trousers*; los pantalones cortos *shorts*

pantis (m pl) *pantyhose*

pañuelo (m) *headscarf*; los pañuelos de papel *tissues*

papá *dad*

papel (m) *paper*; el papel de envolver/ regalo *wrapping paper*; el papel de escribir *writing paper*; el papel higiénico *toilet paper*; los papeles de filtro *filter papers*

paquete (m) *package, packet, parcel*

par (m) *pair*

para *for*; es para mí *it's for me*; para el viernes *by Friday*; ¿para qué? *what for?*; para una semana *for a week*

parabrisas (m) *windshield*

parachoques (m) *bumper*

parada (f) *stop* (bus); la parada de taxis *taxi stand*

parafina (f) *kerosene*

paraguas (m) *umbrella*

parar *to stop*

pared (f) *wall* (inside)

pariente (m) *relative*

parque (m) *park*

parrilla (f) *grill*

parte de atrás (f) *back* (not front)

parterre (m) *flowerbed*

partido (m) *match* (sports); *party* (political)

pasajero (m) *passenger*

pasaporte (m) *passport*; el pasaporte de animales *pet passport*

pasas (f pl) *raisins*

paseo (m) *walk, stroll*; ir de paseo *to go for a walk*

pasillo (m) *aisle, corridor*

paso elevado (m) *overpass*

pasta (f) *pasta*

pasta dentífrica (f) *toothpaste*

pastel (m) *cake* (small)

pastelería (f) *bakery*

pastilla (f) *pill, tablet*; las pastillas de menta *peppermints*; las pastillas para la garganta *cough drops*

patata (f) *potato*; las patatas fritas *french fries, chips*

patinar *to skid*

patines para hielo (m pl) *ice skates*

peatón (m) *pedestrian*

pecho (m) *chest* (part of body)

pedazo (m) *piece*

pedido (m) *order*

pegamento (m) *adhesive, glue*

peinar *to comb*

peine (m) *comb*

película (f) *film, movie*; la película en color *color film*

peligroso *dangerous*

pelo (m) *hair*

pelota (f) *ball*

peluquería (f) *hairdresser*; la peluquería de caballeros *barber*

pendientes (m pl) *earrings*

pensar *to think*; lo pensaré *I'll think about it*

pensión completa *full board*

peor *worse, worst*

pepino (m) *cucumber*

pequeño *little, small*

pera (f) *pear*

percha (f) *coat hanger*

¡perdón! *sorry!, excuse me!* (when sneezing, etc.)

perejil (m) *parsley*

perezoso *lazy*

perfecto *perfect*

perfume (m) *perfume*

periódico (m) *newspaper*

perla (f) *pearl*

permanente (f) *perm*

permiso (m) *license*

pero *but*

perro (m) *dog*

persianas (f pl) *blinds*

pesado *heavy*

pesca (f) *fishing*

pescadería (f) *fishmonger*

pescado (m) *fish* (food)

pescar: ir a pescar *to go fishing*

pez (m) *fish* (animal)

piano (m) *piano*

picadura (f) *bite* (by insect)

picaporte (m) *handle* (door)

picar *to bite* (insect)

picas (f pl) *spades* (cards)

picnic (m) *picnic*

pie (m) *foot*

pierna (f) *leg*

pijama (m) *pajamas*

pila (f) *battery* (flashlight, etc.)

piloto (m) *pilot*

pimienta (f) *pepper* (spice)

pimiento (m) *pepper* (red, green)

pin (m) *PIN*

piña (f) *pineapple*

pinchazo (m) *puncture*

pino (m) *pine* (tree)

pintor (m) *decorator*

pintura (f) *paint*

pinza (f) *peg*; las pinzas *tweezers*

pipa (f) *pipe* (for smoking)

Pirineos: los Pirineos *Pyrenees*

piscina (f) *swimming pool*; la piscina municipal *public swimming pool*

piso (m) *apartment; floor* (story)

pista (f) *runway*

pistola (f) *gun* (pistol)

piston (m) *piston*

pizza (f) *pizza*

plancha (f) *iron* (for clothes); a la plancha *grilled*

planchar *to iron*

plano (m) *town map, town plan;* (adj) *flat, level*

planta (f) *plant*

planta baja (f) *ground floor*

plástico (m) *plastic;* el plástico para envolver *plastic wrap*

plata (f) *silver* (metal)

plátano (m) *banana*

plateado *silver* (color)

platillo (m) *saucer*

plato (m) *plate;* el plato principal *main course;* los platos preparados *prepared meals*

playa (f) *beach*

plaza (f) *site, square* (in town); la plaza de toros *bullring*

pluma (f) *pen;* la pluma estilográfica *fountain pen*

pobre *poor* (not rich)

poco *a little;* poco común *unusual;* poco hecho/pasado *rare* (steak)

poder *to be able*

policía (f) *police*

policía (m) *police officer*

política (f) *politics*

pollo (m) *chicken*

polvo (m) *powder;* los polvos *make-up powder;* los polvos de talco *talcum powder*

pomada (f) *ointment*

poner *to put;* ¿me pone ...? *can I have ...?*

poquito *a little;* sólo un poquito *just a little*

por *through, by, per;* por avión *by air mail;* por la noche *at night;* por noche *per night;* por todas partes *everywhere*

porcelana (f) *china(wear)*

por favor *please*

¿por qué? *why?*

porque *because*

portero (m) *caretaker*

Portugal *Portugal*

portugués *Portuguese*

posible *possible*

postal (f) *postcard*

póster (m) *poster*

postigo (m) *shutter* (window)

postre (m) *dessert*

precio (m) *price;* el precio de entrada (m) *admission charge*

precioso *beautiful* (object)

preferir *to prefer*

pregunta (f) *question*

presupuesto (m) *budget, estimate*

primavera (f) *spring* (season)

primer piso (m) *first floor*

primero *first;* de primera *first class;* primeros auxilios *first aid*

primo (m) *cousin*

prima (f) *cousin*

principiante (m/f) *beginner*

principio (m) *start, beginning*

prisa: tengo prisa *I'm in a hurry*

privado *private*

problema (m) *problem*

producto (m) *product;* los productos de belleza *beauty products;* los productos del hogar *household products;* los productos lácteos *dairy products*

profesión (f) *profession*

profesor/profesora (m/f) *teacher*

profesor/profesora de universidad (m/f) *professor* (university)

profundo *deep*

programa (m) *schedule*

prohibido *prohibited*

prometida (f) *fiancée*

prometido (m) *fiancé*

prometido/prometida (m/f) *engaged* (to be married)

propina (f) *tip* (money)

próximo *next*

prudente *careful*

prueba (f) *test*

público *public*

pueblo (m) *small town, village*

¿puede ...? *can you ...?*

puedo *I can;* no puedo *I can't*

puente (m) *bridge*

puerta (f) *door, gate;* la puerta de embarque *departure gate*

puerto (m) *harbor, port*

pulga (f) *flea*

pulpo (m) *octopus*

pulsera (f) *bracelet*

punta (f) *tip* (end)

puro (m) *cigar*

Q

que *than*

¿qué? *what?*

quemadura (f) *burn*

quemadura de sol (f) *sunburn*

quemar *to burn*

querer *to want, love*

querido *dear* (person)

queso (m) *cheese*

¿qué tal? *how are you?*

¿quién? *who?*

quince *fifteen*

quirófano (m) *operating room*

quisquillas (f pl) *shrimp*

quizás *maybe, perhaps*

R

rábano (m) *radish*

radiador (m) *radiator*

radio (f) *radio*

rápido *fast, quick*

raro *rare* (uncommon)

rastrillo (m) *rake*

rata (f) *rat*

ratón (m) *mouse*

raya (f) *part* (hair)

rebajas (f pl) *sale* (at reduced prices)

rebeca (f) *cardigan sweater*

recado (m) *message*

recepción (f) *reception*

recepcionista (m/f) *receptionist*

receta (f) *prescription*

recibo (m) *receipt*

recobrar algo *to get something back*

recogida (f) *pickup* (postal)

récord (m) *record* (sports, etc.)

recuerdo (m) *souvenir*

redondo *round* (circular)

regalo (m) *gift;* el regalo de cumpleaños *birthday present*

regla (f) *ruler* (for measuring)

reír *to laugh*

rejilla de equipajes (f) *luggage rack*

relajarse *to relax*

religión (f) *religion*

relleno (m) *filling* (in sandwich, cake)

reloj (m) *clock, watch*

remar *to row*

remolque (m) *trailer*

remos (m pl) *oars*

resaca (f) *hangover*

reserva (f) *reservation*

reservar *to book*

resfriado (m) *cold* (illness); tengo un resfriado *I have a cold*

respirar *to breathe*

restaurante (m) *restaurant*

resto (m) *rest, remainder*

retrasado *delayed*;
el autobús se ha
retrasado *the bus is
late*

reunión (f) *meeting*

revelar *to develop* (film)

revista (f) *magazine*

rico *rich*

rímel (m) *mascara*

rincón (m) *corner*
(of room)

riñón (m) *kidney*

río (m) *river*

rizos (m pl) *curls*

robar *steal*; lo han
robado *it's been stolen*

robo (m) *robbery*

roca (f) *rock* (stone)

rock (m) *rock* (music)

rodilla (f) *knee*

rojo *red*

ron (m) *rum*

ropa (f) *clothes*; la ropa
de cama (f) *bed linen*;
la ropa interior
underwear; la ropa
sucia *laundry* (dirty)

rosa (adj) *pink*

rosa (f) *rose*

roto *broken*

rotonda (f) *roundabout*

rotulador (m) *felt-tip pen*

roulotte (f) *camper
trailer*

rubí (m) *ruby* (stone)

rubio *blond(e)* (adj)

rueda (f) *wheel*;
la rueda pinchada
flat tire

rugby (m) *rugby*

ruidoso *noisy*

ruinas (f pl) *ruins*

rulos (m pl) *curlers*

S

sábado *Saturday*

sábana (f) *sheet*
(bedding)

saber *to know* (fact);
no sé *I don't know*

sabor (m) *flavor*

sacacorchos (m)
corkscrew

sacapuntas (m) *pencil
sharpener*

sacar *to bring out*

saco de dormir (m)
sleeping bag

sal (f) *salt*

sala de espera (f)
waiting room

sala de pediatría (f)
children's ward

salchicha (f) *sausage*

salida (f) *exit,
departure*; las salidas
departures; la salida
de emergencia
emergency exit

salmón (m) *salmon*

salón (m) *lounge*
(in hotel)

salsa (f) *sauce*

¡salud! *cheers!* (toast)

sandalias (f pl) *sandals*

sangre (f) *blood*

sartén (f) *frying pan*

sauna (f) *sauna*

secador (de pelo) (m)
hairdryer

seco *dry*

sed *thirsty*; tengo sed
I'm thirsty

seda (f) *silk*

segundo (m) *second*
(noun; adj); de
segunda *second class*

seguro (m) *insurance*;
(adj) *sure, safe* (not
dangerous)

seis *six*

sello (m) *stamp*

selva *rainforest*

semáforo (m) *traffic
lights*

semana (f) *week*;
la semana pasada
last week; la semana
que viene *next week*

seminario (m) *seminar*

semi-seco *medium-dry*
(wine)

señal (f) *deposit*

sencillo *simple*

senderismo (m) *hiking*

señor (m) *Mr., sir*

señora *Mrs., madam*

señorita *Miss*

separado *separated*

septiembre *September*

ser *to be*

serio *serious*

seropositivo *HIV
positive*

servicio (m) *service,
department*; el servicio
de habitaciones *room
service*; el servicio de
radiología *X-ray
department*; el servicio
de urgencias
emergency department

servicios (m pl)
restrooms; los
servicios de caballeros
men's room; los
servicios de señoras
ladies' room

servilleta (f) *napkin*

sesenta *sixty*

setas (f pl) *mushrooms*

setenta *seventy*

seto (m) *hedge*

si *if, whether*

sí *yes*

Sida (m) *AIDS*

siempre *always*

siete *seven*

significar: ¿qué significa
esto? *what does this
mean?*

siguiente *next*

silla (f) *chair*; la silla de
ruedas *wheelchair*

sillita de ruedas (f)
stroller

simpático *friendly*

sin *without*; sin plomo
unleaded

sinagoga (f)
synagogue

sitio (m) *room, space*;
el sitio web *website*

sobre (m) *envelope*

sobre todo *especially*

sobrina (f) *niece*

sobrino (m) *nephew*

soda (f) *soda water*

sofa (m) *sofa*

sofocante *stuffy*

sol (m) *sun*

solo *alone*; yo solo *by
myself*

sólo *just, only*

soltero/soltera (m/f)
single (unmarried)

solución limpiadora (f)
soaking solution (for
contact lenses)

sombrero (m) *hat*

sombrilla (f) *sunshade*

somnífero (m) *sleeping
pill*

somos *we are*

son *they are*

sonreír *to smile*

sonrisa (f) *smile*

sopa (f) *soup*

sordo *deaf*

sostén (m) *bra*

sótano (m) *basement*

soy *I am*; soy de ...
I come from ...

spray (m) *inhaler* (for
asthma, etc.); el
spray antipulgas *flea
spray*

su(s) *its/hers/his/your*
(formal); ¿es suyo
esto? *is this yours?*

subirse *to get in, get on*
(of train, bus, etc.)

sucio *dirty*

sudadera (f)
sweatshirt

Sudamérica *South
America*

sudar *to sweat*

sudor (m) *sweat*

suelo (m) *floor*; el
suelo aislante
groundsheet

sueño (m) *sleep*

suerte (f) *luck*; ¡suerte!
good luck!

supermercado (m)
supermarket

suplemento (m)
supplement

supositorio (m)
suppository

sur (m) *south*

T

tabaco (m) *tobacco*
tabla de windsurfing (f) *sailboard*
tableta de chocolate (f) *bar of chocolate*
tacón (m) *heel* (shoe)
taller (m) *garage* (for repairs)
talón (m) *heel* (foot)
talonario de cheques (m) *checkbook*
también *too* (also)
tampones (m pl) *tampons*
tan *so*; tan bueno *so good*
tanto: no tanto *not so much*; tanto ... como ... *both ... and ...*
tapiz (m) *tapestry*
tapón (m) *cap* (bottle), *plug* (sink)
taquilla (f) *box office, ticket office*
tarde (f) *evening*; (adj) *late*; it's getting late se está haciendo tarde
tarifa (f) *fare*
tarjeta (f) *card*; la tarjeta de banco *bank card*; la tarjeta de crédito *credit card*; la tarjeta de embarque *boarding pass*; la tarjeta de vista *business card*; la tarjeta telefónica *phonecard*
tarta (f) *cake* (large)
taxi (m) *taxi*
taza (f) *cup*
té (m) *tea*
techo (m) *ceiling*
teclado (m) *keyboard*
técnico (m) *technician*
tejado (m) *roof*
tejanos (m pl) *jeans*
tela (f) *material* (cloth)
teleférico (m) *cable car*
teléfono (m) *telephone*; el teléfono móvil *cell phone*
televisión (f) *television*; la televisión por cable *cable TV*
temperatura (f) *temperature*
temprano *early*
tenedor (m) *fork*
tener *to have*; tengo I have; no tengo *I don't have*; ¿tiene? *do you have?*; tengo que irme *I have to go*; tengo calor *I feel hot*; tengo que ... *I must ...*
teñir *to bleach* (hair)
tenis (m) *tennis*
tenue *faint* (unclear)

tercero *third*
terminal (f) *terminal*
ternera (f) *veal*
terraza (f) *terrace*
testigo (m) *witness*
tía (f) *aunt*
tiempo (m) *time, weather*
tienda (f) *store, shop*; la tienda de comestibles *grocery store*; la tienda de discos *record store*
tienda (f) *tent*
¿tiene ...? *do you have ...?*
tierra (f) *land, soil*
tijeras (f pl) *scissors*
timbre (m) *bell* (door)
tinta (f) *ink*
tinto *red* (wine)
tintorería (f) *dry cleaner*
tío (m) *uncle*
tirantes (m pl) *suspenders*
tirar de *to pull*
tirita (f) *adhesive bandage*
toalla (f) *towel*
toallitas para bebé (f pl) *baby wipes*
tobillo (m) *ankle*
toca: me toca a mí *it's my turn*
tocadiscos (m) *record player*
tocar *to feel* (touch)
todavía *yet*; todavía no *not yet*
todo *everything, all*; eso es todo *that's all*
todos *everyone*
todos los días *every day*
tomar *to take*; tomar el sol *to sunbathe*
tomate (m) *tomato*
tónica (f) *tonic*
torero (m) *bullfighter*
tormenta (f) *storm*
tornillo (m) *screw*
toro (m) *bull*
torre (f) *tower*
tortilla (f) *omelet*
tos (f) *cough*
toser *to cough*
tostada (f) *toast*
trabajar *to work* (job)
trabajo (m) *job, work*
tractor (m) *tractor*
tradición (f) *tradition*
traducir *to translate*
traductor/traductora (m/f) *translator*
traer *to fetch*
tráfico (m) *traffic*
traje (m) *suit* (clothing)
tranquilo *quiet*
trapo del polvo (m) *duster*
trasero (m) *bottom* (part of body)

tréboles (m pl) *clubs* (cards)
trece *thirteen*
treinta *thirty*
tren (m) *train*
tres *three*
triste *sad*
tú *you* (informal)
tu(s) *your* (informal); tu libro *your book*; tus zapatos *your shoes*; ¿es tuyo esto? *is this yours?*
tubería (f) *pipe* (for water)
tubo de escape (m) *exhaust*
tuerca (f) *nut* (for bolt)
tuerza (a la izquierda/derecha) *turn* (left/right)
túnel (m) *tunnel*
turismo (m) *sightseeing*
turista (m/f) *tourist*

U

último *last* (final)
ultramarinos (m) *grocer*
un/una *a*
uña (f) *finger nail*
único *single* (only)
universidad (f) *university*
uno *one*
urgente *urgent*
usar *to use*
uso (m) *use*
usted *you* (formal)
utensilios de cocina (m pl) *cooking utensils*
útil *useful*
uvas (f pl) *grapes*

V

vacaciones (f pl) *vacation*
vacío *empty*
vacuna (f) *vaccination*
vagón (m) *car* (train); el vagón-restaurante *restaurant car*
vainilla (f) *vanilla*
vale *OK*
valle (m) *valley*
válvula (f) *valve*
vapor (m) *steam, steamer* (boat); al vapor *steamed*
vaqueros (m pl) *jeans*
varios *several*
vaso (m) *glass* (for drinking)
váter (m) *toilet*
¡váyase! *go away!*
veces: a veces *sometimes*
vegetariano *vegetarian*
vehículo (m) *vehicle*

veinte *twenty*

vela (f) *sailing; candle*

velocidad (f) *speed*

venda (f) *bandage*

vender *to sell*

veneno (m) *poison*

venir *to vome*; ¡venga aquí! *come here!*

ventana (f) *window*

ventas (f pl) *sales*

ventilador (m) *fan (ventilator)*

ventisca (f) *blizzard*

ver *to see*; no veo *I can't see*

verdad *true*; es verdad *it's true*; ¿verdad? *isn't that so?*

verde *green*

verdulería (f) *greengrocer*

verdura (f) *vegetables*

verja (f) *gate*

vestido (m) *dress*

veterinario (m) *vet*

vez: de vez en cuando *occasionally*

viajar *to travel*; viajar en avión *fly (of person)*

viaje (m) *journey*; el viaje de novios *honeymoon*

vida (f) *life*

vídeo (m) *video (film)*; el (aparato de) vídeo *video recorder*

videocámara (f) *camcorder*

vídeo-juegos (m pl) *computer/video games*

viejo *old*

viento (m) *wind*

viernes *Friday*

vigilante nocturno (m) *night porter*

vinagre (m) *vinegar*

vinatero (m) *wine merchant*

vino (m) *wine*

violín (m) *violin*

visita (f) *visit*; las horas de visita *visiting hours*; la visita con guía *guided tour*

visitante (m/f) *visitor*

visitar *to visit*

visor de imagen (m) *viewfinder*

vista (f) *view*

vitaminas (f pl) *vitamin pills*

vivero (m) *garden center*

vodka (m) *vodka*

volar *to fly (plane, insect)*

volver *to come/get back, return*; nos volvemos mañana *we get back tomorrow*

voz (f) *voice*

vuelo (m) *flight*

W, Y, Z

web site (f) *website*

whisky (m) *whiskey*

y *and*

ya *already*

yo *I*

yogur (m) *yogurt*

zanahoria (f) *carrot*

zapatería (f) *shoe store*

zapatilla (f) *washing machine*

zapatillas (f pl) *slippers*

zapatos (m pl) *shoes*; los zapatos de deporte *athletic shoes*

zona peatonal (f) *pedestrian zone*

zoo (m) *zoo*

zumo juice (m); el zumo de frutas *fruit juice*; el zumo de naranja *orange juice*; el zumo de tomate *tomato juice*

Acknowledgments

The publisher would like to thank the following for their help in the preparation of this book: Isa Palacios and Maria Serna for the organization of location photography in Spain; Restaurant Raymon at Mi Pueblo, Madrid; Magnet Showroom, Enfield, London; MyHotel, London; Peppermint Green Hairdressers, London; Coolhurst Tennis Club, London; Kathy Gammon; Juliette Meeus and Harry.

Language content for Dorling Kindersley by G-AND-W PUBLISHING
Managed by **Jane Wightwick**
Editing and additional input: **Cathy Gaulter-Carter, Teresa Cervera, Leila Gaafar**

Additional design assistance: **Lee Riches, Fehmi Cömert, Sally Geeve**
Additional editorial assistance: **Paul Docherty, Lynn Bresler**
Picture research: **Louise Thomas**

Picture credits

Key:
t=top; b=bottom; l=left; r=right; c=center; A=above; B=below

p2 **Alamy:** *ImageState / Pictor International;* p4/5 **Alamy RF:** *Image Source tl;* **Alamy:***D Hurst bl;* Indiapicture bl; p10/11 **Alamy RF:** *BananaStock tl;* **Getty:** *Taxi / James Day cbl;* **Ingram Image Library:** *bl;* p12/13 **Alamy RF:** *Dynamics Graphics Group / Creatas cBr; John Foxx cAr; RubberBall br;* **DK Images:** *cl;* **Ingram Image Library:** *tl, cr;* p14/15 **DK Images:** *tcr;* **Ingram Image Library:** *cl, cBl, cAr, cBr, bcr;* p16/17 **Getty:** *Taxi / James Day bcr;* **Ingram Image Library:** *tcr;* p18/19 **DK Images:** *David Murray tr;* p22/23 **DK Images:** *cl, Andy Crawford cAr; Susanna Price br; Magnus Rew tcrB;* **Ingram Image Library:** *tcr;* p24/25 **DK Images:** *clA, Dave King br;* p26/27 **Alamy RF:** *Dynamic Graphics Group / Creatas cl;* p28/29 **DK Images:** *John Bulmer tcr; Dave King cr; Matthew Ward bcl;* **Ingram Image Library:** *bcrA, bcr;* p30/31 **Alamy:** *Comstock Images bcl Think Stock bclA;* **DK Images:** *cl;* p34/35 **Ingram Image Library:** *tcr;* p36/37 **DK Images:** *bcl, bcr; Magnus Rew cl;* **Ingram Image Library:** *bl;* p38/39 **Alamy RF:** *Imageshop / Zefa Visual Media cl;* **Ingram Image Library:** *cr;* p40/41 **DK Images:** *Peter Wilson bl;* **Lee Riches:** *cl;* p42/43 **Alamy RF:** *Image Source tr, cAr, cAAr;* p44/45 **Alamy:** *Jon Arnold Images br; ImageState / Ethel Davies bl; Vikki Martin cbl; Peter Titmuss bcrr;* **Alamy RF:** *Iain Davidson Photographic bcll; David O'Shea bcr; Courtesy of Renault:* c; p46/47 **Alamy RF:** *Imageshop / Zefa Visual Media cr;* **Ingram Image Library:** *cr; Courtesy of Renault: tcrB;* **Lee Riches:** *bcl;* p48/49 **Alamy:** *Balearic Pictures c;* **Alamy RF:** *Brand X Pictures bcl;* **DK Images:** *tcr, bcl; Neil Lukas br; John Miller crA;* **Lee Riches:** *cl;* p50/51 **Alamy:** *Peter Titmuss cr;* **Lee Riches:** *c;* p52/53 **Alamy:** *Jean Dominique Dallet tcr;* **Alamy RF:** *Image Farm Inc cAr; Imageshop - Zefa Visual Media tcrB;* **DK Images:** *cl;* p54/55 **Alamy:** *Jackson Smith cBl;* **Alamy RF:** *Brand X Pictures cl; John Foxx c; Image Source cAr; ThinkStock tcr;* **DK Images:** *Andy Crawford bcl;* p56/57 **Alamy:** *Balearic Pictures clA;* **Alamy RF:** *Brand X Pictures clAA;* **DK Images:** *cl; Neil Lukas tl; John Miller tcll;* **Lee Riches:** *tcl; Courtesy of Renault: bc;* p58/59 **Alamy:** *Michael Juno tr;* **Alamy RF:** *Brand X Pictures cBl, cBBl; Ingram Publishing cAAl;* **DK Images:** *cAl; Max Alexander cBr;* p60/61 **Alamy:** *Robert Harding Picture Library bcr;* **Alamy RF:** *Image Source cAr;* **DK Images:** *Steve Gorton bl, tcrB; Pia Tryde cAAr;* **Ingram Image Library:** *cr;* p62/63 **DK Images:** *Stephen Whitehorn tr;* p64/65 **Alamy:** *Arcaid bcrA; Mike Kipling c;* **Alamy RF:** *GKPhotography cBr; Goodshoot cAr; Justin Kase tcrB;* **DK Images:** *Steve Tanner cl;* **Ingram Image Library:** *tcr;* p66/67**Alamy:** *Arcaid tl;* **Alamy RF:** *Ingram Publishing cAr;* **DK Images:** *tr; Stephen Whitehorn bl;* **Ingram Image Library:** *br;* p68/69 **Alamy:** *Balearic Pictures cr; directphoto.org cAr; Doug Houghton cl; Indiapicture clB;* **Alamy RF:** *CoverSpot cBl;* **Lee Riches:** *cr;* p72/73 **Alamy RF:** *imagebroker tcl bl; Image Source cAr; Comstock Images cr;* **Avery Weight-Tronix:** *bl;* p74/75 **Alamy RF:** *Doug Norman bl;* **Ingram Image Library:** *cr;* p76/77 **Alamy:** *Balearic Pictures clA; Indiapicture bl;* **Alamy RF:** *Coverspot clB;* p78/79 **Alamy RF:** *Luca DiCecco bcl; Steve Hamblin br;* p80/81 **Getty:** *Taxi / Rob Melnychuk bc;* **Ingram Image Library:** *cAr;* **Xerox UK Ltd:** *tcr;* p82/83 **Alamy:** *wildphotos.com tcr;* **Alamy RF:** *FogStock cAAl; Momentum Creative Group cAl; Shoosh / Up the Res cBl;* **Ingram Image Library:** *cl;* p84/85 **Alamy:** *Brand X Pictures cr; fl* **Alamy RF:** *BananaStock bl; Comstock Images c; SuperStock tr;* **Ingram Image Library:** *crB;* p86/87 **Alamy RF:** *Luca DiCecco br;* **Getty:** *Taxi / Rob Melnychuk tc;* p90/91 **Alamy RF:** *Brand X Pictures cr;* **DK Images:** *cl; David Jordan cbl; Stephen Oliver cr;* **Ingram Image Library:** *cBr;* p92/93 **Alamy RF:** *Pixland cr;* **DK Images:** *cl; Guy Ryecart tr;* p94/95 **Alamy:** *David Kamm cl; Phototake Inc bcl;* **Alamy RF:** *Comstock Images cr; ImageState Royalty Free bcr;* **DK Images:** *Stephen Oliver tcr;* p96/97 **Alamy RF:** *Pixland br;* **Ingram Image Library:** *tr;* p98/99 **Alamy:** *Andrew Linscott c; Shotfile cr;* **Alamy RF:** *Bildagentur Franz Waldhaeusl bl; ThinkStock br;* p100/101 **DK Images:** *Steve Gorton tcr;* p102/103 **Alamy:** *Hortus b; D Hurst tcrB;* **Alamy RF:** *image100 tcr; Barry Mason cAAr;* **Ingram Image Library:** *cAr;* p104/105 **DK Images:** *Paul Bricknell cl(6); Jane Burton bcl; Geoff Dann cl(2); Max Gibbs cl(4); Frank Greenaway cl(3); Dave King cl(1), cAr; Tracy Morgan cl(5);* p106/107 **Alamy:** *Shotfile cr;* **Alamy RF:** *Barry Mason br;* p110/111 **Alamy RF:** *Think Stock cr;* **DK Images:** *Andy Crawford cl;* p112/113 **Alamy RF:** *Dynamic Graphics Group / Creatas tcr; image100 bl;* **Ingram Image Library:** *cl; bcrA;* p114/115 **Alamy:** *John Cole cr;* **Alamy RF:** *Image Source cAr; Index Stock cAl; jackhollingsworth.com tcr;* p116/117 **Alamy RF:** *Dynamics Graphics Group / Creatas clA; John Foxx clB;* p118/119 **Alamy:** *D Hurst tcr;* **Alamy RF:** *Pixland tcr;* p120/121 **Alamy:** *ImageState / Pictor International cl; Shotfile cBl;* **Alamy RF:** *Sarkis Images tcr;* p122/123 **Alamy RF:** *BananaStock cl;* **Ingram Image Library:** *cl;* p124/125 **Alamy:** *ImageState / Pictor International bclA; Shotfile cBl;* **DK Images:** *bcl; Paul Bricknell tc(5); Geoff Dann tc(3); Max Gibbs tc(1); Frank Greenaway tc(2); Dave King tc(4); Tracy Morgan tc(6);* **Ingram Image Library:** *bl;* p126/127 **Alamy:** *Jean Dominique Dallet cl;* **Alamy RF:** *Imageshop - Zefa Visual Media blA; Image Farm Inc bl;* p128 **DK Images.**

All other images **Mike Good.**